Making Sense of the Intercultural

In this book we wish to find a new way of talking about, connecting and operationalising the third space, narratives, positioning and interculturality. Our purpose is to shake established views in what we consider to be an urgent quest for dealing with prejudice.

We therefore seek to draw attention to the following:

- how Centre structures and large culture boundaries are sources of prejudice
- how deCentred intercultural threads address prejudice by dissolving these boundaries
- how, in everyday small culture formation on the go, the cultural and the intercultural are observable and become indistinguishable
- how agency, personal and grand narratives, discourses, and positioning become visible in unexpected ways
- how we researchers also bring competing narratives into making sense of the intercultural
- how third spaces are discordant and uncomfortable places in which all of us must struggle to achieve interculturality

This book is therefore a journey of discovery with each chapter building on the previous ones. While throughout there are particular empirical events (interviews, reconstructed ethnographic accounts and research diary entries) with their own detailed analyses and insights, they connect back to discussion in previous chapters.

Adrian Holliday is Professor of Applied Linguistics & Intercultural Education at Canterbury Christ Church University, UK.

Sara Amadasi is a post-doctoral researcher at the University of Modena and Reggio Emilia, Italy.

Making Sense of the Intercultural

Finding DeCentred Threads

Adrian Holliday and
Sara Amadasi

Routledge
Taylor & Francis Group

LONDON AND NEW YORK

First published 2020 By Routledge

2 Park Square, Milton Park, Abingdon, Oxon OX14 4RN
605 Third Avenue, New York, NY 10017

Routledge is an imprint of the Taylor & Francis Group, an informa business

First issued in paperback 2022

Publisher's Note

The publisher has gone to great lengths to ensure the quality of this reprint but points out that some imperfections in the original copies may be apparent.

British Library Cataloguing-in-Publication Data
A catalogue record for this book is available from the British Library

Library of Congress Cataloging-in-Publication Data
A catalog record has been requested for this book

ISBN: 978-1-138-48203-6 (hbk)
ISBN: 978-1-03-233766-1 (pbk)
DOI: 10.4324/9781351059190

Typeset in Times New Roman
by Deanta Global Publishing Services, Chennai, India

Contents

Preface

The purpose of this book is to present different ways of thinking about old concepts. Much has already been written about the Centre, the third space, narratives, positioning, interculturality and so on. In this book we wish to find a new way of talking about, connecting and operationalising these concepts. Our purpose is to shake established views on what we consider to be an urgent quest for dealing with prejudice. Small culture formation on the go becomes a useful site in which the interconnection between these concepts can be seen and empirically analysed in new interconnections. It therefore becomes the new alternative to large cultures as a starting point for sense-making – starting from the inside out, beginning with what can be seen rather than what is imagined. Working in this way reveals huge uncertainties, and we do not claim to simplify anything as we engage with the complex realities that emerge throughout the book.

We therefore seek to draw attention to the following:

- how Centre structures and large culture boundaries are sources of prejudice
- how deCentred intercultural threads address prejudice by dissolving these boundaries
- how, in everyday small culture formation on the go, the cultural and the intercultural are observable and become indistinguishable
- how agency, personal and grand narratives, discourses, and positioning become visible in unexpected ways
- how we researchers also bring competing narratives into making sense of the intercultural
- how third spaces are discordant and uncomfortable places in which all of us must struggle to achieve interculturality

This book is thus a journey of discovery with each chapter building on the previous ones. While throughout there are particular empirical events (interviews, reconstructed ethnographic accounts and research diary entries) with their own detailed analyses and insights, they connect back to discussion in previous chapters. Chapter 1 presents the theoretical underpinning, a map of the book, in Table 1.1, and a glossary of key terms, which are therefore contextualised by the first empirical event that opens the chapter. In Chapter 2, we explore instances of prior research, not because we are preoccupied with the research events *per se*, but because they represent first-hand experience of small culture formation on the go and how we researchers are participants, with our own competing narratives, in co-constructed research. The implication of this unexpected complexity for the realisation of threads is then explored in Chapter 3; and in Chapter 4, we two authors explore each other's research trajectories to get behind what is going on between ourselves and the people we are researching. This prepares the ground for the finale in Chapter 5.

Throughout, Sara's specialism in interaction analysis is complemented by Adrian's reconstructed ethnographic accounts and email interviews. These interacting methods take form within a broad constructivist ethnographic approach. We take material from primary school and migration settings, study abroad, and postcolonial fiction; but we are not doing a study of any of these *per se*. They are scenarios where we have observed crucial instances of behaviour which speak to the overall issue of the intercultural. Therefore, we do not claim a book that *belongs* to primary education, migration studies, study abroad or postcolonial fiction. Nevertheless, what we have to say about the intercultural and the origins of prejudice will have relevance for readers from all of those areas, plus health and social care, business and management studies, internationalisation in universities, cultural studies and so on. We hope that the book resonates with a growing understanding that many specialist and institutional issues connect with the everyday experience of culture and identity.

Transcription conventions

In conversation extracts, the following conventions are used where it is important for the analysis: - without a space in front for abrupt breaks or stops; (.) when the speaker makes a pause; (0.2) for the number of seconds the pause is lasting; ((all rise hands up)) to indicate behaviour within the interaction; […] to indicate that some of the original words were cut. These are used mostly with the conversations with children in Chapter 2, where there is more detailed interactional analysis.

Acknowledgements

We would like to thank Claudio Baraldi, Claudia Borghetti, Katarzyna Gasiorowska, Malcolm MacDonald, Vittorio Iervese, Amina Kebabi, Asmaa Madagh, Amira Oukraf, Yasmine Sadoudi, Alexander Seale, Nour Souleh, Juman Simaan and Ismatul Zaharin, Wafa Zekri. They listened, gave us ideas and corrected us. Sara thanks all the children she met during her PhD research for what she learnt from them. Fouad Mami introduced Adrian to Laila Lalami. Adrian's grandchildren, Aara and Anoushiravan, demonstrated intercultural research. At Routledge, Nadia Seemungal and Elizabeth Cox provided continued support. Colleagues at conferences and seminars in Bologna, Helsinki, Leeds, Lisbon, Modena, Southampton and Darmstadt provided a community of discussion.

1 Distant lands and the everyday

In this book, we try to move how we think of the intercultural to another place. The core concept of deCentring involves pulling away from the established, false, Centre notion of bounded, homogenous, separate, large cultures associated with nation, ethnicity and religion. We follow much critical sociology in defining the Centre as interrelated dominant structures, discourses and narratives which define and reproduce a world order. We characterise large cultures as Centre forces because they impose structures which confine and reduce people, who are presumed to be contained by them, to prescribed stereotypes. It is for this reason that we write this book to attempt a demonstration of how deCentring the intercultural is necessary if we are to address the prejudices that arise from these Centre, large culture forces. DeCentring the intercultural in no way denies diversity, but refuses to bind it in large culture blocks.

We do this by reflecting on the play of narratives and positioning in instances of small culture formation on the go. These are a series of empirical events which involve children with migration backgrounds, university students abroad and ourselves, in interaction within interviews, workshops and reconstructed ethnographic accounts. While these participants have particular features, they represent all of us everywhere.

To underpin this task, we employ an alternative, postmodern understanding of a truer, hybrid, shifting nature of culture, where imagined large culture boundaries are known to be ideologically constructed.[1] This framing of the conflicting understandings of culture is inspired largely by Gerd Baumann's (1996) ethnography of the London Borough of Southall, where references to culture are multiple and creative, dependent on who is speaking to whom and about what. While this non-essentialist notion has

---

1 We have moved away from the distinction between solid and liquid cultures (Dervin 2011, citing Bauman) because while solid implies boundedness in a very definite sense, liquids also have boundaries, albeit more fluid.

achieved some recognition (MacDonald & O'Regan 2011), discourses of bounded homogeneity continue to be deeply ingrained in persistent narratives of culture that surround us both in the academy and in everyday life (Holliday 2018c; Holliday & MacDonald 2019). This is why moving how we think to a hybrid, shifting, unbounded, non-essentialist mode is a constant struggle and requires far more than the normal change in understanding. In the writing of this book, we acknowledge the fear and dismay that can arise when we pull away from Centre structures, and our inability to face and accept the true complexity of social life. This does not mean that we should not try to pull away, faced as we are by the prejudices towards others that we see around us every day.

In the words of Kuhn (1970), it is part of an ongoing paradigm revolution through which deeply established Centre discourses have constantly to be shaken. Framing this paradigm shift as deCentring is thus a way of signalling the seriousness of what needs to be done.

As the book is about the deCentring of the *inter*cultural, we are not therefore writing about the interaction between perceived 'members' of separate bounded homogenous cultures. Indeed, within the unbounded hybrid perception of culture it is hard to distinguish between the intercultural and the cultural. Our core concept of small culture formation on the go is the basic site for engaging with culture from an early age wherever and with whomever we are. Speaking of *the* intercultural rather than the more common 'intercultural communication' signals a state of being rather than a movement between – perhaps indeed of always being rather than just when we are travelling to distant places – which recognises a cultural diversity and perhaps discord everywhere as the first step in the interculturality of finding ourselves in others and others in ourselves. Recognising that everything cultural is also intercultural is a way of alluding to the natural ambivalence and hybridity of who we all are at all times.

Here it is worth noting that the concept of hybridity has had different readings. Essentialist readings have been that it is an in-between space between homogenous cultures (Fairclough 2006: 25). The non-essentialist, deCentred reading is very different. Stuart Hall states that 'new identities of hybridity' are replacing 'national identities' for all of us (1996a: 619), Homi Bhabha that it is the nature of culture *per se* (1994: 56), Delanty that it is the nature of the cosmopolitan (2006: 33), and Guilherme that it represents an 'upsurge of new forms of life' (2002: 128). It is this reading that helps us to understand also the third space, not as an in-between, temporary place where bounded and homogenous cultures can be negotiated, but as where we need, perhaps uncomfortably, always to stand if we are to see the hybrid complexity of things.

This first chapter will attempt to unravel these concepts, upon which the rest of the book will then develop its discussion. However, because we want theory to emerge from direct observation, we will begin with an event. The choice of this event grew out of we two authors asking each other what happened in our lives that set us off thinking the way that we do about the intercultural. While it is therefore based on something real that happened to one of us, we present it as a fictionalised, reconstructed ethnographic account. In such accounts throughout the book, we say neither where the characters come from nor in which countries the events are located. This is both to maintain anonymity and to help focus on small culture processes without being seduced by large culture imageries. Applying this ethnographic discipline of making the familiar strange makes us try hard to put these imageries aside. By shifting whatever our personal knowledge of whichever of us the character might be to another persona also helps us to enter into a less comfortable third space from which we can have another view of what might be going on. We have made Kati ambivalent about the concepts of 'white' and 'European' to disturb the event in which we place her.

Kati in Exia[2]

The following is a reconstructed ethnographic account of an incident experienced by a young anthropology student named Kati during a study visit to Exia. It introduces a number of key elements of the book. It is an instance of small culture formation on the go, where, in a passing encounter, she reflects on how she is positioned and positions herself within a wider cultural environment. Her intervention into her own thinking disturbs what might have become her dominant narrative of what she thinks is going on and therefore takes her into a deCentred third space. Kati is a fictional character who will reappear throughout the book, based upon a number of people we researchers have interviewed or observed.

> That evening Kati ate a mango in the Exian countryside. Actually, she ate a lot of mangos in Exia, but this one was linked to a meaningful moment that frequently came into her mind in conducting her research work years after.
>
> It was an evening in August and it was already dark. One of those evenings of the rainy season when everything seems uncertain because a storm might arrive suddenly. Kati and her group were used to eating

2 Exia is a fictitious name for a country that is constructed as exotic by those who visit it, as used by Holliday (2011, 2018c) where it is important to indicate such a country without naming an actual place.

all together in the centre of the courtyard under a gazebo that hosted all the social events taking place inside the village association that was hosting her.

That evening, after dinner, she was sitting alone in a corner of that same gazebo when her friend, Diak, came and sat next to her with this mango in his hand. He cut it into sections and they shared it, in silence, spending some minutes there, eating the mango without saying a word.

Kati did not speak his language, but had learnt French at school, and could therefore speak it with him and the people of the village who had also had the chance to study it. Although Diak spoke poor French, he usually tried his best to narrate his stories to her. They came to know each other through music. Some evenings, after dinner, he put his mobile phone in the middle of the courtyard and played music while everyone was chatting or looking at the sky above the savannah. Other times, after lunch, he took Kati's mp3 player, put on the earphones and spent his time just listening to the music, with intense curiosity in his eyes.

The silence of that evening was not due to anything related to being speakers of different languages though. That silence was rather a new but perfect language between Diak and Kati that was perfectly suited to that specific moment. The next morning he had to leave the village, to start a new life in Europe. And while Kati was sad to see her friend leaving, she could also perceive how he wasn't hiding from her his fear for this new experience and the sadness of leaving the village and the friends he grew up with.

If we think about migration as the human need to move somewhere else to find things you do not have in the place you usually reside, be it money, love, work or knowledge, Kati could also consider herself a temporary migrant in those days. She had left two months before to study transnational migration in that village, moving to a place she had never been before and whose language she did not speak. Of course, there were differences between their experiences and she was aware of this. For example, unlike Diak, she already had a return ticket, while he did not know when he would be able to return.

But in those months she came slowly to realise how she was an object of observation and prejudice from the people around, which in some moments, made her really feel a foreigner there. The first and easiest way through which people defined her was her being 'white' and a woman, though in other places there were people who she knew considered themselves 'white' in contrast to her. She certainly didn't consider herself 'European', which was what the word they often used for her seemed to mean.

She knew that these things happen everywhere, because every individual risks falling into the trap of Othering, as well as being Othered. But it was exactly finding herself in the position of being Othered that made her start to understand the relevance of creating a space with people around to let the other know more about who you are, to push knowledge beyond the surface of categories and to manifest yourself as a specific person, with all your contradictions and layers of complexities.

She thus started to try to look at herself with the eyes of the people around her; and she felt this deep need to claim a space of interconnection with them, to increase the possibility of cutting across the categories of 'foreign student' and 'Exian hosts'.

As soon as this dichotomy was evident to her and she intervened to disturb it, she realised that, while she was thought to be the one who was there to observe, she was actually the object of the study of the people she met, with no exception of Diak himself, who, while demonstrating curiosity about her journey and the place she had left, was preparing his departure with discretion, and without revealing his plan until the very last days.

It was not just on the evening of the shared mango, but on the evenings after, when Diak had already left and his funny jokes were no longer populating the courtyard, that Kati clearly understood how they had both something to study and explore in the other, but that this was not due to being 'members' of different cultures. It was instead linked to the resemblance between the experiences they were living or approaching to live, each one with its peculiarities, but, at the same time, similar in their way of involving the circuits of common feelings.

We have started with this event to demonstrate how an apparently simple and innocent event can disturb the common narratives that we construct to make sense of what we are doing, and to lead us into a deCentring perspective in which new meanings can be tested and investigated. Despite language and different national backgrounds and Kati's perceived distance from the people of the village, Diak's sharing of his story with Kati created the possibility of a thread that began to dissolve expected large culture boundaries. The unexpectedness of this thread, and the fact that Kati had to work to re-align her own positioning before she could appreciate it, brought the kind of disturbance necessary for it to be deCentred. It was a deCentred thread because it succeeded in interrupting the flow of her view about the intercultural and imposed a shift in her way of looking, constructing and reproducing narratives about relations with others. The new, disturbed perception of what was going on around her, that enabled the emergence of this thread, is what we refer to as a third space.

Main events, storyline and concepts

What Kati experiences in this event is far from straightforward. The difficulty required in explaining it is necessary because we wish above all else to avoid easy answers, which we feel have contributed to past misunderstandings of the intercultural.

Each chapter is therefore organised around a series of events that we need to struggle to explain. These are taken from our observation of intercultural life; and they are in dialogue with the ideas that we formulate around them. They represent the experiences that lead us to form our agendas in writing this book. The events are described in Table 1.1. They take the form of face-to-face (I) or email interviews (E), workshops (WS), reconstructed ethnographic accounts (RE), research diary entries (RD) and discussion of literary fiction (F). While most of the events are with school children and study abroad students, these are taken as examples of everywhere, our

Table 1.1 A summary of events and storyline

Chapter	Events	Storyline
1: Distant lands and the everyday Setting the scene, storyline and concepts	Kati in Exia (RE) Matt and a woman on the train (RE) Lalami's *The Moor's Account* (F)	*We reconstruct an early epiphanous experience of the intercultural that set us off on the quest for **deCentred threads**.* Kati realises that **threads** can be formed despite foreignness, in languages that are foreign to everyone. She has to work to **position** herself carefully. It pleasantly *disturbs* her comfortable reality. It becomes a **deCentred third space**. *We then look at an everyday experience.* Matt encounters an annoyingly noisy woman on the train. He thinks her behaviour is because she is foreign and has not integrated into 'his culture'. After talking to Kati, he works hard to **reposition** himself – to **deCentre** himself to interrogate his prejudices. He then sees the woman as just noisy and annoying. *We then look at how hard it is to get to the **third space** even though it is everywhere.* Layla Lalami has to reconstruct a sixteenth century story of extreme displacement and foreignness to find a **deCentred third space** where the narratives of colonialism are revealed. Showing that this story is about all of us all the time indicates that the **third space** can be a normal **deCentred** space.

Chapter	Events	Storyline
2: DeCentred threads resist the expected	Sara and Children with migration backgrounds (WS, RD)	*We discover the unexpected politics of **positioning** by looking at what leads up to workshops that were carried out with the participants.* When Sara carries out workshops with children with migration backgrounds she finds **threads** that, differently to the dominant discourse, show they are expert cultural travellers. However, Sara's research diary and detailed interaction analysis of the setting up of the workshops reveals that the children's expertise is unexpectedly in how they *resist* Sara's **positioning** and bring her to a **deCentred third space**. Threads therefore emerge from apparent discordances. *This contributes to a major theme of the book, that people are never what they seem to be and that small culture formation on the go is open – that its importance is in its discordance.*
3:Centred threads become blocks	Kati and Eli talking about blocks and threads (RE) Sara and Adrian talk to Wissaal about clothes (I) Kati going to a 'foreign' place with Eli and Matt (RE)	*We explore how **threads** can easily become **blocks** if they are not **deCentred**.* Kati and Eli have several conversations about each other's attitudes towards where they are studying abroad and where they come from. They discover that there are prejudices hidden in their own critique of the **blocks** of others and in their own **threads**. Following what we learn about our own researcher implicatedness in the politics of **positioning**, we show **blocks** and **threads** in how we talk to a postgraduate student abroad and to each other about cultural artefacts and clothes. Kati and Eli experience how they and Matt form **blocks** and **threads** in unexpected ways.
4: Who are we researchers?	Sara and Adrian talking to each other (I) Postgraduate researchers talking (E, I)	*Having seen how we researchers are implicated in forming **threads** and **blocks** in small culture formation on the go, we explore the intercultural resources we take this from.* We experience uncomfortable **third spaces** in **deCentring** ourselves as we talk to each other about **threads** and also discover how we create personal **blocks**. We then explore how postgraduate researchers abroad also share these struggles in their trajectories. *It becomes clear that all of us, whether researchers or the people we research, are caught up in discordant negotiation of who we are.*

(Continued)

Table 1.1 Continued

Chapter	Events	Storyline
5: Getting on with deCentred life	[5] Kati and the song (RE) An unexpected and positive conclusion	*We conclude with the unexpected discovery of a deCentred grand narrative. This confirms the trajectory of the book in understanding that deCentring is at the core of finding threads that dissolve essentialist boundaries and also at the crucial margins of our experience.* Kati is taken to a completely unexpected place by undergraduate students that she teaches. As with the children in Chapter 1, **deCentred threads** come from their initial resistance to her teaching. Out of them seeming uninterested in issues of migration, they show her the **deCentred** 'getting on with life' grand narrative.

focus being on the commonalities of the intercultural rather than on specific aspects of education. They are opportunistic in the sense that these are incidents and instances that we happened to have encountered and then selected on the basis of having sufficient richness of interaction and access, and of having resonance with what we have seen before and what we are looking for. They are also examples of everywhere and everyone.

Glossary

While all of these and other key concepts will be described in detail and developed below and throughout the book, it might be helpful to provide a short glossary here:

- **Positioning** is what we all do to adjust our stance in relation to people, interactions and ideas.
- **Threads** are resonance we create to connect with others. They need to be deCentred to avoid being blocks.
- **Blocks** are resonances we create that relate to Centre narratives and discourses that construct boundaries between ourselves and others.
- Things are **deCentred** when they resist Centre narrative and discourses.
- A **third space** is a place where normality is sufficiently disturbed to enable us to deCentre.
- **Small culture formation on the go** is the primary intercultural location where we all engage with, construct, resist or change culture every day – which is small enough and big enough for positioning, threads and blocks to be visible.

- **Interculturality** is the quality we all potentially possess to enable deCentred threads.
- **Narratives** are stories that we construct or draw from as we position ourselves and make blocks or threads, **grand** when they construct the, usually, Centre image of the world and which speak ideology, **personal** when they are our own, but sometimes splintered from the grand.
- **Discourses** are the language formations, spoken and visual, with which narratives are expressed.

These concepts and their definitions are complex and contestable and will be expanded and adapted as they are used, interconnected and discussed throughout the book.

Investigating the dynamics of small culture formation *on the go*

Small culture formation on the go is where people come together to construct culture on a daily basis. Small cultures are any social arrangement where two or more people come together to make or negotiate culture and could range from established social groupings such as a department, a social club or a family, to an event such as a meal or a meeting.

However, the notion of 'on the go' pulls away from too much focus on the location. We are less concerned with the specifics of particular groupings than with the 'on the go' dynamics of small culture formation everywhere. 'On the go' implies the transient and sometimes discordant nature of how people everywhere engage: coming, going, accepting, rejecting, remaking, breaking, passing by, upsetting and disturbing; being in conflict with others and the norms of the 'group' or cultural place; accepting, resisting or challenging social conventions through interactional choices. This is where small culture formation on the go is different from Wenger's (2000) more normative community of practice, which implies some form of development of a functional group. The small culture is not a normative product, but rather an environment in which the intercultural takes place, and hopefully where interculturality can come about. In the ethnographic account at the beginning of this chapter, Kati's interaction not just with Diak eating the mango, but with the people of the village she is visiting, is a good example of this. We only have her own thoughts in the account; but we can see her making sense also of potential discordance in the way she imagines people seeing her.

Figure 1.1 indicates that small culture formation on the go is where the negotiation of narratives takes place. The top and right domains of the figure indicate the Centre and the unrecognised margins that are defined and

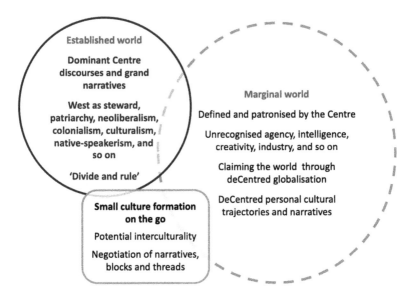

Figure 1.1 Centre and margins

patronised by the Centre. These narratives can be either the grand narratives of the Centre or the personal narratives of deCentred personal cultural trajectories. Because small culture formation on the go is based on underlying universal cultural processes that are shared by everyone, it has the potential to act against the Centre desire to define and divide who we are. It can do this by tapping into the memories of intercultural experience that provide the threads that can dissolve Centre boundaries. The phrase 'divide and rule' is often used to describe how British colonial powers maintained power by turning the people they ruled against each other. The Centre structures that are generated by dominant discourses and grand narratives, as listed in the figure, are well-known also to tend to do this. Neoliberalism, as discussed later, tends to segment processes so that they can be justified through quantification; colonialism and culturalism have histories of separating an imagined 'deficient' Other from an imagined 'civilised' Self; native-speakerism defines as essentially different imagined 'non-native speakers' and 'native speakers' along similar grounds (Holliday 2018b); and patriarchy builds its power on imagined essentialist gender roles.

The figure takes elements from Holliday's (2018c) grammar of culture, where small culture formation and personal cultural trajectories, while being the areas most often ignored by the positivism of large culture studies, are at the core of what all of us bring to the intercultural. While there is therefore a clear connection between small culture formation on the go and deCentred narratives in the marginal world, the necessary threads might not always be appreciated. The reasons for this will be explored throughout the book, especially in Chapter 3. Small culture formation on the go therefore has the potential for interculturality; but the narratives and discourses of the established world are sufficiently seductive and intrusive for this not always to happen. Other details in the figure will be explained as the chapter continues, especially in the section on critical cosmopolitanism.

The notion that personal cultural trajectories and narratives are commonly structured originates in email interviews with people from a range of cultural backgrounds, all of whom spoke similarly about their diverse cultural identities as formed and changing through cultural travel (Holliday 2010; 2011: 41–68). However, the note of caution about vulnerability derives from the uncomfortable fact that these personal narratives can also be essentialised through influence from Centre grand narratives – so that small culture formation on the go can be pulled back to the Centre. We also need to be cautious about what we mean by 'shared by everyone' in this respect. The processes of small culture formation on the go are shared in the sense that they involve underlying universal cultural processes. Some of these processes however lead us to be taken in by, and to adopt, essentialist Centre narratives that have the appearance of dividing us – for example 'my culture is different to yours because we don't do this'. Such narratives are also shared in the *structure* of their discourses – i.e. to essentialise, in the sense that we all essentialise, whereas their narrative *content* might not seem shared. In this sense, both Centre and deCentred discourses and narratives can be shared at particular levels of generality.

Small culture formation on the go is therefore our site of investigation because it is where the employment of diverse and often conflicting narratives can be seen – how narratives are chosen and employed, and how blocks and threads are created. We can switch between these narratives, minute-by-minute, as we position ourselves in different ways depending on what we encounter. 'On the go' also emphasises our concern with what emerges from these narratives at the moment of interaction rather than with expectations related to the participant's cultural background.

The openness of small culture formation on the go means that when people come together there is a multiplicity of things going on that open up many possibilities for how narratives can intertwine and express themselves. It is this transient and often discordant process that reveals the deeper nature of how we position ourselves and are positioned. In the Kati and the mango event, we can see Kati positioning herself with two competing narratives, one of the pleasure of being together and one of conflict around how she feels she might be being received by the village. We will say more about blocks and threads, positioning and narratives below.

Small culture formation on the go is not only a device for seeing what is going on. It is something that is there anyway, wherever we look. The small culture formation on the go approach to cultural travel and interculturality includes all parties, both already there and arriving, passing by and staying for long or short periods, as part of the local and negotiate positionings and narratives that contribute to cultural flux.

Because small culture formation on the go takes place from an early age, as soon as children begin to engage with social life, it provides the basic experience that all of us can use to travel to new cultural environments. It provides the major experiential resource in any intercultural setting. Understanding that it is therefore a process in which everyone is expert helps us appreciate the expertise of all parties within research settings.

Negotiating blocks and threads, developing interculturality

Blocks are essentialist references to large cultures as though they are separate and mutually exclusive bounded and homogenous entities that define everything about who we are. Threads pull in the opposite direction. They are non-essentialist connections in our lives, thoughts and experiences that dissolve large culture boundaries. They reside in personal narratives that draw on personal cultural trajectories. Threads become a space where deCentring is possible and where the unexpected can disturb expectations and pre-established roles. As we will see below, while roles are legitimised by structures, fluid positions are created, taken up or abandoned in relation to the interactional context. For this reason, it is by focusing on positionings, both in the interactional event as well as in the analysis, that threads become not only empowered, but observable in their development.

Therefore, an area where threads can be found is within the concept of interculturality. This term has been used in recent years to depict the quality that enables positive and creative intercultural engagement. An established definition is 'a dynamic process by which people draw on and use the resources and processes of cultures with which they are familiar but also those they may not typically be associated with in their interactions with others' (Young & Sercombe 2010: 181). Dervin (2016: 103–106) says that it is a highly creative quality that requires the reflexive and uncertain work of digging beneath the surface of discourses and politics. The reflexive and creative nature of interculturality is at the core of the creative yet sometimes discordant nature of small culture formation on the go. Its uncertain and perhaps uncomfortable nature also fits with the core concepts of deCentring and third spaces.

In the Kati and the mango event, Kati is constructing several threads to help her connect with the villagers: eating the mango, speaking a French that is in different ways foreign to all of them, sharing music, enjoying silence, the anxiety of travel to unknown places. At the same time there is a threat of an essentialist block that she imagines around their perceptions of 'foreign student' and 'Exian hosts'.

However, the nature of blocks and threads and the relationship between them is far from straightforward, as shall be demonstrated in Chapter 3; and this complexity contributes to that of small culture formation on the go as discussed above, where negotiating blocks and threads are a major mechanism.

Narratives, positioning and social action

By narratives, we mean stories that are present in the wider cultural environment that people draw upon in their daily lives (Amadasi & Holliday 2017: 259, citing Somers and Baker). 'Grand narratives' are those that we inherit and are brought up with – the big stories that are designed to define our heritages and to legitimate the social groups we are part of. They are part of the 'cultural resources' attached to 'particular social and political structures' in Holliday's grammar of culture. They are also the basis for Holliday's 'global position and politics' category, through which we inherit the stories of nation and race that position us in relation to the cultural Other. They are fed by essentialist ideologies of nation and race and realised through established discourses of culture. They are ideological in that they contribute to how we orientate our thoughts about the world; and, indeed, they are promoted by the ideologies of race, gender and culture. While, in the postmodern turn, they may have lost their credibility as indisputable truths, they live on in the manner in which governments, markets, institutions, and indeed all social groups and individuals spin, construct and reconstruct their images (Botting 1995; Goodson 2006). Even though we may be critical of grand narratives, their residues are persistent and pervasive in different permutations and splinters in the way that we all think about our lives (Lyotard 1979: 22).

In the Kati and the mango event, her fear of a foreign-student-Exian-host block draws in an existing 'us'-'them' grand narrative of colonisation which both she and the villages are aware of. It is waiting there to be invoked as an explanation for any form of discord that might develop between them, and is so powerful that it can turn Kati into a 'white' European even though she does not see herself as such.

Personal narratives are those that we form ourselves through everyday experience, and which guide our actions (Somers 1994). In this respect, 'personal cultural trajectories', as referred to above, are a core element of Holliday's grammar of culture because they mediate and filter how we respond to the structures within which we are brought up.

Our reference to grand and personal narratives is similar to what Somers (1994) identifies as ontological and public narratives. However, differently from her theorisation, our interest is in the intertwining and overlapping of grand and personal narratives in individuals' accounts. As grand narratives are part of the wider environment that we interact with, the splinters of grand narratives are thus irrevocably present in our personal narratives (Mannheim 1936: 52). We have varying degrees of awareness of the presence of grand narratives as, through these splinters, we employ aspects of the discourses that express them between the lines of everyday experience (Fairclough 1995; Wodak & Meyer 2015). In this sense, personal narratives can be volatile as they help us make shifting sense, solve the ever-changing daily problems of identity, and sometimes pick up essentialist splinters to express cultural blocks, or reach out to others with non-essentialist cultural threads. The overall picture therefore is of complex, multi-faceted and shifting plots. It is however a choice, in the interactional events, for participants to draw upon grand narratives or to leave space for more personal narratives. This choice will have effects on the course of events, affecting other participants' choices, in a chain of action and reaction sequences. We need to remember that, without evidence of what any of the villagers might think, it is Kati's personal narrative which invokes the Centre colonial grand narrative that she initially uses to explain the discord of how she believes that they relate to her. She then has to be shaken out of this Centre interpretation by the interaction with Diak, before she can build an alternative personal narrative that includes the thread with his experience.

Narratives thus can be often in conflict with each other as they bring essentialist, divisive blocks or non-essentialist threads that dissolve boundaries. As we shall see in Chapter 2, the research setting, and in particular the conversational interview, is an excellent place to see these processes unravelling. It is itself an example of small culture formation on the go; and it shows how the researcher is implicated in the employment of conflicting narratives while at the same time able to intervene to foster threads that support interculturality. To see more clearly what is going on in the interview it is necessary to look more widely at the bigger social canvas from which we choose the narratives we employ – the media, education, global position and politics, and personal cultural trajectories.

There is an *agency* implicit in how we draw on these narratives which reflects the social action theory of Max Weber (1964) where, given the circumstances, we can be in creative dialogue with the grand narratives implicit in the social structures of nation and its attendant ideologies and discourses. We all make choices in how we position ourselves in intercultural interaction by employing and switching between the different grand and personal narratives that are available to us. We need to be clear that Kati *chooses* a personal narrative that splinters from a colonial grand narrative before she then *chooses* to pursue the alternative personal narrative that recognises a deCentred thread.

Together with narratives, interactional *positioning* also plays an important role in small culture formation on the go. Positioning can be defined as 'unfolding narratives' (Amadasi & Iervese 2018: 245) in communicative events in which speakers take up, reject, confirm or negotiate (Amadasi 2016; Harré & Van Langenhove 1999: 19–20) the choices, the acting out of which legitimises narratives, which in turn legitimises positional interactional choices. While every act of positioning implies a 'cluster of rights and duties' (Henriksen 2008: 43) which partially constrain us, they are dynamic and subject to situational changes and negotiation processes which take shape inside social interactions (Henriksen 2008: 42) and therefore defy static role-based theories about situational behaviour (Amadasi & Iervese 2018). Positionings are therefore relational and mutually independent. By positioning ourselves, we invoke positionings for our interlocutors (Baraldi 2009: 6) who can confirm or reject them. Positioning is therefore social in the sense that the discursive constructions of personal stories are legitimated and explained through and inside a more complex network of personal and collective narratives.

Therefore, whatever is going on between Kati and the villagers, her thoughts indicate that she is positioning herself in particular and also complex ways as she applies threads, imagines blocks and invokes narratives.

Constructivist, ethnographic research

We employ whatever methods necessary to get to the bottom of what we are looking at, but all within a unifying, broadly ethnographic approach in which rigour is claimed through the application of the disciplines of: allowing meaning to emerge from direct observation; making the familiar strange; researchers constantly being aware of and interrogating their own positionality; and carefully constructing thick description by juxtaposing instances of social life to create a larger detailed picture of what is going on. The epistemological underpinning of this approach derives from the postmodern turn in qualitative research which acknowledges the subjective implicatedness of researchers as interactants in the research event (Clifford & Marcus 1986). It is constructivist in the recognition of the social construction of reality (Berger & Luckmann 1979) and the co-construction of positioning and narrative negotiation within small culture formation on the go.

This has particular relevance for the research event, which we perceive as itself an example of small culture formation on the go, where the researchers themselves 'cannot, in a sense, write stories of others without reflecting' on their 'own histories, social and cultural locations as well as subjectivities and values' (Merrill & West 2009: 5). Interviews, such as those which feature in the coming chapters, and indeed the conversations which take place within workshops in Chapter 2, are also sites where all parties jointly co-construct meanings and make sense of the world (Miller 2011; Talmy 2011), and 'potentially creative space[s] between people' (Merrill & West 2009: 114). They are transient, interactive social spaces where all parties become momentary members even though some of them may never have taken part in such events before. As with any small culture setting, interviews and research conversations involve diverse role definitions, hierarchies, individual positions, formalities and informalities, loyalties, variable lines of power and responsibility, and multidirectional senses of duty that can be tacit, blurred and dependent on event. They are particularly apt sites for researching the intercultural because all parties make a conscious attempt to inhabit spaces and construct deliberated narrative statements.

These points also relate to the whole thick description that we form in the intertwining of data from research diary entries in Chapter 2, extracts from blog posts in Chapter 3, and the reconstructed ethnographic accounts used throughout the book. These are places where we researchers make a reflexive note of what we understand about the research setting at or near the moment of observation. Indeed, such entries and reconstructions are a record of how we position ourselves in the form of a personal narrative with regard to what we see around us. They are indeed the living record of instances of small culture formation on the go between we researchers and the people and events in the settings we observe.

The reconstructed ethnographic accounts are validated through the full application of broadly ethnographic discipline. While they are constructed stories, they are faithful to observed behaviour; and the characters are led to interact in such a way that the meanings that they construct must begin to take on a life beyond the expectation of the researcher and author. The construction of the narratives borrows from the notion of creative non-fiction as described by Agar (1990: 77–78), where the researcher demonstrates how social situations develop through interaction between composite characters and events which are based on prior ethnographic observation. They have been used in a number of previous publications (Holliday 2011, 2018c). The original inspiration is Kubota's (2003) 'Unfinished knowledge: the story of

Barbara' in which she manages to skilfully describe the complex and non-essentialist nature of culture, and also Arundhati Roy, who puts aside the positivist notion that writers 'cull stories from the world' (2002, track 3). We do not therefore only analyse stories as relevant for the understanding of social processes, but as social processes themselves – stories which surround us all, and in the construction and production of which we researchers cannot help but actively participate. Latour explains this well when he says that social scientists should 'just offer the lived world and write', providing 'reflexive accounts' which give relevance to their own stories instead of getting lost in arguments which feed back on themselves and risk nullifying their own claims (1988: 175).

Critical cosmopolitanism

The postmodern paradigm has also produced a critical cosmopolitan argument (Delanty, Wodak & Jones 2008), supported by critical and postcolonial sociology (Bhabha 1994; Hall 1991; Said 1978), that it is a Western grand narrative that has falsely defined and marginalised non-Western cultural realities, as indicated in the marginal world in Figure 1.1. Holliday (2016a: 32ff) has framed this process of Othering as an apparently well-wishing though in reality deeply patronising West as steward discourse. It recognises complexity and fluidity in social processes and the multiple ways through which the social world is constructed in different contexts with different modernities (Delanty 2006) and acknowledges that cultural realities are built at an individual level around individuals' personal circumstances that dissolve structural and spatial boundaries (Beck & Sznaider 2006: 383; Holliday 2011: 61). A sense of the West as steward discourse can be seen in the reference to 'host Exians' noted by Kati in the ethnographic account at the beginning of the chapter. The term 'host' can signify the recipients of aid or educational help which hides colonialist patronage and racism under a veneer of apparently well-wishing care and education. It is culturally relativist in that it presumes that the cultural Other requires either protection or special care because its values and practices are incompatible with 'ours'. The discourse is embodied in the common phrase of apparent praise that cultural migrants can find so aggressive: 'You are doing so well' – to be like us, and to get rid of your past, so quickly.

This sociological perspective hints at the possibility of a deCentred cosmopolitan person. We can see this in the way that Kati tries to make sense of her position within the village that she is visiting. While she notes the possibility of a blocking colonial grand narrative, she tries to think through this, not taking for granted and even denying her position within discourses about being 'white' and 'European', and trying to *intervene* 'to disturb it', at least in her own mind, by acknowledging that she was being observed and not just the observer. This critical cosmopolitan lens on Kati represents a focus on how participants present and refer to their own stories rather than conferring on them pre-determined identity features. We do not refer to participants' life stories as psychological accounts but rather as stories that they create in response to the particular contextual and interactional resources that they encounter. Kati therefore, along with our ethnographic account of her experience, is not just expressing an 'us-them' narrative about her own national cultural background. Indeed, taking the core sense of social action from Holliday's grammar of culture, her personal cultural trajectory develops there and then to include her new experience and a reassessment of who she is and where she comes from.

DeCentring intervention in third spaces

Bringing all of the above to bear, the intervention that we focus on in this book is to encourage the taking of action and the making of choices to recognise and negotiate competing narratives for the purpose of overcoming essentialist blocks and finding non-essentialist threads. This relates both to our 'participants', which we see as a clumsy label for the people we encounter in interviews and other research events, more simply described as Italian school children with migration backgrounds and postgraduate study abroad research students, and to ourselves as researchers who are also implicated in narrative negotiation as we interact with them.

The research events in this book are therefore sites of small culture formation on the go in which *all* the people taking part are agents of intervention who respond to each other's interventional choices. The reconstructed ethnographic accounts are a demonstration of how other actors, embodied by Kati and her friends, also engage in intervention in negotiating narratives to deal with blocks and to find threads.

There is some resonance here with work on identity formation and intervention in interview settings in recent studies of intercultural conversations, given that we now understand that this is no longer something that happens between people from separated bounded large cultures. However, whereas they look specifically at how communicative forms of intercultural learning (Borghetti & Beaven 2018) and forms of interaction (Baraldi 2014b) are performed, our focus is more on what forms of narratives emerge within the broader remit of small culture formation on the go. The reconstructed ethnographic account at the beginning of this chapter is an example of the latter, where we see Kati struggling with how to intervene in how she interacts with the people she is visiting to overcome the blocking colonialist grand narrative and a West as steward discourse of culture.

The reason that we insist on this intervention being deCentred is that this is the only way to make it work in the face of the immense power of the Centre narratives, and the discourses of culture that support them, in maintaining blocking grand narratives. In our use of the term 'deCentred', we take inspiration from Stuart Hall, where he says that:

> The most profound cultural revolution has come about as a consequence of the margins coming into representation ... not just to be placed by the regime of some other, or imperialising eye but to reclaim some form of representation for themselves. ... Marginality has become a powerful space. It is a space of weak power but it is a space of power ... the discourses of the dominant régimes, have been certainly threatened by the de-centred cultural. ... The subjects of the local, of the margin, can only come into representation by, as it were, recovering their own hidden mysteries. They have to try to retell the story from the bottom up, instead of from the top down.
>
> (1991a, 34–35)

Along with this postcolonial setting for deCentredness, we also take guidance from a second statement, by bell hooks, where she describes the state of mind of the margins:

> To be in the margin is to be part of the whole but outside the main body. ... We could enter that world but we could not live there. We had always to return to the margin, to cross the tracks, to shacks and abandoned houses on the edge of town. ... There were laws to ensure our return. ... Living as we did – on the edge – we developed a particular way of seeing reality. We looked both from the outside in and from the inside out. We focused our attention on the centre as well as on the margin. Our survival depended on an ongoing public awareness of the separation between margin and centre and an ongoing private acknowledgment that we were a necessary, vital part of that whole. This sense of wholeness, impressed upon our consciousness by the structure of our daily lives, provided us an oppositional world view – a mode of seeing unknown to most of our oppressors, that sustained us, aided us in our struggle to transcend poverty and despair, strengthened our sense of self and our solidarity.
>
> (1984: i)

Both of these statements relate to what might be considered the permanent struggles of particular groups of marginalised people who are fighting for recognition against the Centre. What makes hooks' statement particularly poignant is that the Centre also comprises women who are 'bourgeoise' feminists and 'not opposed to patriarchy' (hooks 1984: 7). This brings the intersection of race into the picture. Hence, we have the colonised in Stuart Hall's statement, and racialised black women in hooks', with the Centre being the West and patriarchy respectively.

The scenarios in our book are far less obvious examples of marginalised realities struggling for recognition against a Centre that Others them through reducing them to imagined cultural deficiency. As stated at the beginning of the chapter, we are concerned with Centre structures that inhibit the cultural realities that dissolve bounded and homogenous culture boundaries. The critical cosmopolitan sociology we discussed in the last section emphasises that these realities are personal and hidden by such structures. Perhaps the classic example of this, which connects with the West as an inappropriate definer of 'the Rest' as suggested by Stuart Hall (1996b), is the Orientalism thesis as set out by Edward Said (1978). He states that the cultural realities of the East were imagined rather than understood by the West. This imagination was driven by projections of the Western Self – an idealised image of 'us' that constructed 'them' as opposite and inferior. The Orientalism thesis can also be extended to the mis-defining of the South by the North. Its power is that these demonised images of the Other are present everywhere – in the way that we are educated, in every part of our media, in our art and literature and in our histories. The 'our' here does not refer only to the Western gaze, but to everyone in the sense that these imaginations have been implanted in everyday dominant experience across the world.

The implication of this is that Kati, wherever she comes from, will have been brought up, educated, and influenced by media, politics, even advertising and so on, with grand narratives that marginalise and reduce the Exian Other. This is why, for her even to begin to overcome these blocks and find threads, she has to deCentre herself – to find ways of extracting herself from the discourses, such as the West as steward discourse, that underpin these essentialist narratives. We feel that she begins to do this by locating herself as not 'white' or 'European' and thinking about how she might be Othered by the people she is with.

The need to deCentre the Orientalist gaze also underpins the postmodern, constructivist research methodology described above. It is now well-known that the purpose of the more traditional, positivist anthropology and ethnography has in the past provided such narratives about an imagined deficiency of colonised 'cultures' for the purpose of finding rationales for colonialism (Clifford 1986).

The deeply sustained nature of this Centre large culture perspective can be connected to what Beck and Sznaider (2006: 4–5), among others, refer to as a 'methodological nationalism'. This, influenced by nineteenth century European nationalism, reifies nation, with matching language and culture, as a 'socio-ontological given' and the default starting point for social science and popular perception. To counter this default homogenising of nation, language and culture, we find useful C Wright Mills' (1970) concept of sociological imagination as a means to stand critically within a wider perspective of history and ideology that can hopefully see through and around confining Centre structures.

While deCentring is a process of seeing differently, we maintain that third spaces are where it happens. The notion of third space has been much discussed in intercultural studies, with a wider range of discoursal orientations (Holliday 2018c: 138, 145; MacDonald 2017). Our reading of third space is different to the common perception that we frame as essentialist where, we feel, it has been falsely constructed as a temporary, intermediate space between two essentially incompatible large culture blocks, and where the cultural traveller therefore negotiates who they are 'in between' their own and the new cultures. This construction is also implicit in the more established notion of interculturality, which is limited to a 'critical awareness of the Other', of a separate place 'over there', which implies 'learning about who we are compared to "them"' and 'being tolerant of "their" values'. Kumaravadivelu (2007: 5), as an Indian academic living in the US, is particularly critical of this essentialist construction of the third space because it leaves him 'dangling in cultural limbo', which he by no means feels he is. There is a strong implication that the Self can never therefore really ever be the Self without negotiated concessions in terms of cultural practices and values.

The non-essentialist version of the third space, which we promote, is quite different in that it is everywhere all the time and a *normal* space in the same sense that it is normal to be a cultural traveller. It resonates with what (Delanty 2006: 33) refers to as a place where 'new relations of self, other and world develop in the moments of openness'. Homi Bhabha argues that the third space, as framed in this way, 'entertains difference without an assumed or imposed hierarchy' (1994: 5) by escaping the Centre 'fixity' of colonial discourse (94) and 'politics of polarity' so that we can all 'emerge as others out of selves' (56).

It may seem strange that the 'normal' is also 'new'. This for us is the nature of the conundrum around the concept of deCentred. It is there all the time in the sense that it has to do with the realities that are there all the time but that are hidden or distorted by the Centre grand narratives that do not recognise them – in effect, the discourses of hierarchy, polarity and colonial fixity.

We would therefore hope that Kati in the Exian countryside does not think of herself in some sort of temporary in-between space because she is away from home and yet not belonging in her new location. The threads that she creates though silence, music, the shared anxiety of travel and the speaking of French, which is foreign to her and the Exian villagers, are resources that she has both brought with her and also found there. It is her discovery that she can also find these resources, and indeed a continuation of her personal cultural trajectory among people who have hitherto been strangers, that will disturb her established thinking sufficiently to be deCentred and to intervene in, and upset, her existing thinking-as-normal.

The third space is therefore a normal space where:

- Self and Other can be found in each other
- interculturality is explored and discovered
- the nature of the Centre and the deCentred can be laid bare in order to achieve this
- exploration and discovery takes place
- the workings can be seen in small culture formation on the go.

It is a site for looking and searching for the deCentred and is also at the core of interculturality.

Matt and the woman on the train

The second event in this chapter demonstrates more precisely how finding non-essentialist threads through a deCentred third-space intervention was attempted in a more everyday event. It therefore responds to the title of the chapter – distant lands in event one resonating with everyday 'home' events. The following reconstructed ethnographic account is of what happened to one of Kati's friends, Matt, while travelling on a train. We express it as a series of acts to indicate the progress being made in Matt's coping and engagement with what happens:[3]

Act 1: Essentialist blocks

Matt was beginning a three-hour train journey when he found, sitting across the aisle from him, a woman whom he perceived to be 'foreign' from her appearance, language and behaviour. He found her particularly annoying because she was having a very loud phone conversation that went on and on and on. Moreover, her phone was on speaker and he could also hear the also very loud voice of the person she was talking to.

---

3   This account is based on a real experience of one of the authors, but also on how we all often construct prejudicial theories about others on the basis of their appearance.

His first response was to construct an essentialist block by theorising that she came from a 'collectivist' culture that had no regard for personal space. He took this from something he had been reading on cultural difference as part of his university course. He had also read that we should tolerate people from other cultures because they couldn't be expected to understand 'our values'. Nevertheless, he couldn't get out of his mind that she really should learn that people in 'this country' respected personal space. Then he thought that this woman might be not well-socialised into living here because she only mixed with her own people and was therefore isolated and culturally confused.

Act 2: Finding deCentred third-space threads

He had to tell someone about what was going on. He texted his friend Kati who had come there to do a masters in intercultural studies. She had told him a lot about her recent time in Exia as part of her previous anthropology course. She had already told him that he shouldn't take seriously the out-of-date cultural profiling stuff because it was neo-racist and that he should know better as a student of cultural studies.

By now he'd moved to another seat and could still hear the woman talking from half-way down the carriage even when he was listening to music on his headphones. Kati texted back that he needed to look at himself, to stop being so racist and to think about what he'd been telling her about the Stuart Hall and bel hooks he'd been reading. She said that he needed to interrogate his own well-wishing patronage and lingering patriarchy that Westerners seemed to carry with them wherever they went.

When she texted, 'why do you think she's foreign anyway?', he recalled the group of foreign-looking people walking along the platform with huge suitcases, also making lots of noise in 'their language' and almost pushing people out of their way. He'd thought at the time that he needed to get rid of these racist images. Anyway, why did he even think that she was associated with them?

So, he began to recall other stuff too. It wasn't just foreigners who'd invaded his space. Boys at school teased him because he refused to use bad language which he could now associate with what women called 'misogyny'. On his course they'd looked at how the media, advertising and school textbooks implanted racist images.

He began to think that he was indeed concocting a theory about the Other just to help him position himself against this totally annoying woman. He also began to excavate his own patriarchal tendencies. Yes, it would have been just as annoying if it was a man making all the noise;

but there was also something lurking in his theorising about how this woman needed instruction about how you don't need to speak into a cellphone so loudly and how not to have it on speaker mode by mistake.

He texted some of these reflections back to Kati. She eventually replied that she hoped that all this soul-searching didn't mean that he was now going to excuse the woman's behaviour, because that would also be patronising. She texted that culture, and also gender, should never be an excuse. Yes, she was just an annoying person on a train.

The points we wish to make about this event connect the distance implied in the account of Kati in Exia with the most ordinary and everyday nature of this one. Even in the ordinary and everyday there is intervention that takes Matt into a third space – an uncomfortable space where he begins to deCentre himself. Perhaps, as is the case in many reconstructed ethnographic accounts, where other characters provide critical tension, he did need, however, to talk to someone else to set him off on this difficult quest. Even though he had read more critical literature about culture, race and gender, he had initially chosen the neo-racist literature that is still very much available to help him explain what was going on. This is an example of how Centre narratives can be so deep-set and powerful that we can forget evidence and education that opposes them. The literature he referred to is also seductive because it pretends well-wishing. It relates to a cultural relativist discourse in which acknowledging that 'members' of particular large cultures have characteristics that prevent them from being or doing what 'we' prefer is framed as somehow protecting of them. This relates to the concept of culture being an excuse – for example, 'we can't expect X to support the rights of women because their culture doesn't permit it'. We think that this viewpoint is patronising; and where it is subscribed to by X themselves it is what Kumaravadivelu (2012: 60) refers to as self-marginalisation. It is an 'imagined marginalised world' which the Centre uses to excuse its own patronage, but which has also become so powerful that it has been bought into by those whom it marginalises (Holliday 2016a: 32; 2018c: 128).

The 'getting on with life' grand narrative

It would be quite easy to imagine that grand narratives are bad and the major source of essentialist blocks. To do so would be to fall into the methodologically invalidating trap of only finding what we set out to look for. Instead, we feel it is a major success of our methodology that we were able to come by accident upon a grand narrative that seemed to do the opposite. We then realised that this was what we were unknowingly looking for all along. The 'getting on with life' grand narrative emerged as a result of the events that inspired the writing of the final chapter. We perceive it to be a non-essentialist, thread-forming grand narrative that survives when we are not threatened or invaded by divisive grand narratives. What we need to think of as an outcome of its discovery is how to recover it, and where it resides. While we do not introduce the 'getting on with life' grand narrative until Chapter 5, having it in mind as a possibility helps us to keep open all options as we explore what is going on in small culture formation on the go and not jumping to conclusions about what is possible. It is a grand narrative that makes it possible to think of a prejudice-free and boundary-dissolving humanity. Thinking of this helps us to place our research participants as the protagonists of social events and choosing subjects in their own intercultural journeys, and thus cultural innovators. Readers may wonder why we do not begin with the unexpected example of this narrative as a contextualisation for the rest of the book. We can say, however, that we have introduced the possibility here sufficiently to put it into the minds of readers as they work through the ensuing chapters.

Getting to the deCentred: *The Moor's Account*

In the last part of this chapter we will look in more detail at the concept of deCentredness and third space from the opposite spectrum to the woman on the train event. Instead of the normality of everyday life in the current period, we will look at the normality of a distant time and place and extreme displacement. We will also revisit the nature of cultural travel as something that is not confined by or between particular times and places, but which is multidirectional. The woman on the train event shows that for Matt to travel what we might consider 'forward' to reconsider the woman's behaviour, he has to travel 'backwards' into his own orientations to deCentre his perceptions. This resonates with Holliday's (2016c) revisiting of the common notion of intercultural competence; he talks about how he has to pull threads from the past into making sense of new encounters, and the core tenet of his grammar of culture is that the intercultural experience that we all bring with us is our major resource for forging threads with the new and strange.

The normality of the cultural traveller

The discussion about whether or not cultural travel is mono- or multidirectional has to do with how far it is normal to be a cultural traveller and how to find the deCentred within this normality. An unexpected analysis to help us to get to the bottom of this question can be found in the postcolonial writer, Laila Lalami's (2015) novel, *The Moor's Account*. The novel is set in the early part of the sixteenth century. Moroccan Mustafa ibn Muhammad sells himself into slavery to survive European economic expansion. He is then taken on a Spanish colonial expedition to the Florida and Texas hinterland in 1527. The expedition is beleaguered by the indigenous population to the extent that only a few of the Spanish conquistadors remain and are enslaved along with Mustafa. Because Mustafa has medical expertise, he is employed as a travelling doctor by their captors and he becomes the protector of the men who had enslaved him.

Not only are the tables turned and the slave-master relationship problematised, with Mustafa's prior masters becoming his friends who depend on his new-found status for their safety, but both he and they find unexpected but 'normal' humanity among the indigenous people. Indeed, 'they live in sophisticated towns and decide their affairs by consultation' (Lalami 2015: 268).

As Mustafa and his Spanish now-dependents wander from town to town with his work, they eventually come to the border of the established Spanish colony of Mexico. As they return to 'civilisation', there is heightened ambivalence about their original slave-master relationship. Also, Mustafa, as the 'strangely' senior member of the four survivors, is asked by the colonial authorities to give a detailed account – the 'Moor's account' – of the territories and people that they have seen. The problem is that, to justify Spanish invasion of these territories, they want him to say that the people there are sufficiently 'uncivilised' to justify colonisation. They demand descriptions of populations in need of education and conversion, where, for example, 'they kill their own infants' and 'treat their women like beasts' (269). Mustafa feels unable to do this. Somehow, the continued ambivalence in the relationship with his prior masters leads them to protect him from having to do this.

What Lalami makes very clear in the novel is that the 'problem' with cultural travel is not the people who travel or the 'cultures' to which they travel, but the narratives that surround this relationship. The colonial authorities want to colonise; but they cannot do this without what they consider to be justification. To get this justification, they need a narrative about the people they wish to subjugate. In her review of the novel, Crown (2015) notes that it is 'a thoughtful investigation into how we frame the narratives of our own lives', and how Mustafa himself notes how, among the Europeans, 'just by saying that something was so, they believed that it was. I know now that these conquerors … gave speeches not to voice the truth, but to create it' (Lalami 2015: 10).

Crown's linking of this story of the extreme deprivation of colonisation, slavery and displacement to the experiences of all of us is of immense importance. Being able to see this connection is at the core of our discussion in this book. It is the fact that this connection can be made that clarifies the normality of cultural travel – that what happens to Mustafa, and indeed his colonial masters, can resonate back to very ordinary experiences in everyday life. One might argue that it is a trick of the novelist to create resonances across time. On the other hand, such resonances could not be created if the reader did not have the experience to meet them. Stylistics will have something to say about this with reference to schemata, which is beyond the scope of this book. The possibility of this connection is what will make deCentring possible. In the woman on the train event, it is what allows Matt to connect events across his life with the experience of the supposedly foreign woman speaking too loudly. Across fiction and film we are able to identify with psychedelic characters across worlds and universes.

Centre, deCentre and positioning

There are of course a large number of narratives at play throughout the telling of this story. To indicate something of the complexity, Table 1.2 presents an analysis of the three narratives in Lalami's novel, as noticed and defined

Table 1.2 Narratives and positioning

Narratives	Centre-deCentre forces	Positioning
Noting how, among the Europeans, 'just by saying that something was so, they believed that it was. I know now that these conquerors … gave speeches not to voice the truth, but to create it'	DeCentred witnessing of the Centre discourse	Mustafa's education in how to maintain his deCentred positionality Also perhaps recognised from his own Centre preoccupations at home
'They live in sophisticated towns and decide their affairs by consultation'	DeCentred reality	Subscribed to: by Mustafa who is already deCentred through slavery and is himself struggling to be seen like this by the conquistadors who are shaken out of Centre master-slave relationships and experience unexpected realities
'They kill their own infants' and 'treat their women like beasts'	Centre colonialist imagination Mirrors Centre Orientalist preoccupations	Presented to Mustafa as a condition for him joining the Centre He resists to maintain his deCentredness He recognises it from his own past

by ourselves and Crown. Relationships with Centre and deCentre are used in the analysis as an operational sounding point to see where this takes us. They provide a basis for the positionings in the final column.

What seems worthy of note is that Mustafa is able to position himself critically against Centre narratives because he is colonised, and because he has seen them in his own pre-colonised life experience. This helps make the point that the Western colonising Centre is not the only Centre. An equally powerful Centre, that can be found in societies across the world, which we might imagine that Mustafa is familiar with, is patriarchy – which also marginalises and hides the cultural realities of women with grand narratives of their deficiency. An interesting and rather extreme example of how a patriarchal system, which is often there under the surface, can come into play at times of panic is in Sardar's (2009: 132–133) reference to the Baradari, or brotherhood, system in British communities with roots in a particular part of Pakistan, with occasional recourse to forced marriage. I mention this not to add to the common essentialist criticism of 'Asian culture', but to draw attention to how Centre structures can operate unseen in the background. Sardar's point is that modern families can appear liberal regarding things like marriage arrangements and may not realise that patriarchy is there until conflicts of interest arise. People can choose the marriage partners that they prefer, even under the heading of 'arranged marriage', where families operate as convenient dating agencies. However, if the choice steps out of what the community accepts, the patriarchal system springs into fierce action. I do not think that we have to be British Pakistani to have at least distant experience of something like this. Even males can suffer the consequences of being subject to patriarchal hierarchies. At a very simple level, Matt, in the woman on the train event, can feel himself as a male marginalised by other males in a patriarchal hierarchy with which he is complicit, but to which he also falls victim.

Being shaken out of one set of structures, as the conquistadors are (mid right column), will undoubtedly heighten awareness of all structures. Coming back to the resonance with everyday life, as we move through the multiple structures of family, work, education, employment, marriage and so on, and their attendant and also shifting narratives and discourses, we do not have the extremes described by Lalami, but we might feel considerably displaced in relative terms. For all of us, Centre structures are fierce forms of control, even if for most of the time they remain invisible. This does not mean that we do not have choices. Even the slave has the choice to remain silent while waiting for the right opportunity to do otherwise. This choosing to be silent is exemplified in the film, *Twelve Years a Slave* (McQueen 2013), in which the protagonist does not mention his identity before being enslaved until he meets someone who might have the power to act effectively on his behalf.

The neoliberal Centre

The core of the Centre discourse of 'just by saying that something was so, they believed that it was' (top left in the table) resonates strongly with what we now refer to as neoliberalism. Indeed, perhaps it *was* some sort of neoliberal thing that was going on even in Lalami's fictionalised sixteenth century colonialism. There too, externalised rationalities needed to be provided to give an impression of morality – to show external bodies, in their case the colonial establishment, that they were caring about people while being financially viable in exploiting conquered lands. This locating of neoliberalism in the distant past can also be seen in the (2018) television fiction, *Britannia*, about the Romans invading Britain. The Roman general talks to the community leaders he is about to enslave about 'partnerships and taxes'. This role of politics as an 'imaginary' to help us only to remember what is convenient for the current order and to forget what is not convenient is well expressed by Stuart Hall (1991: 52).

There is also resonance here with the current neoliberal agenda in which institutions and policy are supposed to view 'international' students under the established heading of 'internationalisation'. The agenda has to fit established thinking and quantify and specify how students are educated in self-determination and critical thinking so that there is a clear sense of 'value added'. Indeed, neoliberalism has become another Centre for many university researchers, where the actual language that they can use in research projects has to be modified to sound more positivistic, quantifiable and even essentialist to meet the requirements of funding agencies (Collins 2017; Cribb & Gewirtz 2013; Holliday & MacDonald 2019; Kubota 2016). One reason why Matt clings to old essentialist concepts in the woman on the train account while he is also exposed to more critical, non-essentialist literature, might be that the former may just seem more established and 'normal'. This is what encourages us to stay with stereotypes that 'need no evidence' (Homi Bhabha 1994: 94).

What it takes to listen to the deCentred

It is the 'Moor's account' that is the focus of Lalami's novel – an account that is deCentred because it refuses to conform to the expected Centre grand narrative that foreigners were in need of civilising colonisation. For us to get to listen to and understand this unexpected account, a story of massive cultural displacement needs to be told. For us, it is the Moor's deCentred account that we have to get to if we are to get to the core of an interculturality that is rooted in the everyday small culture formation on the go that we all have in common regardless of where we come from and where we are going.

However, Lalami provides us with a way *through fiction*. We have to think what it takes to allow fiction to be evidence. Here it is useful to be reminded of Stenhouse's (1985: 31) statement that reading the novel *Madame Bovary* can tell us more than a 'survey of 472 married women'. Lalami does this with a fictional auto-ethnography from 'the Other'. This is resonant with the accounts of postgraduate researchers in Chapter 4, which they employ to research their own experiences as 'international' students. Lalami provides us with a long and fully contextualised, inter-subjective journey to see ourselves from another place. We see there what Mustafa has to go through to get to the story about all humanity that everyone knows but no-one believes. It is the Centre neoliberal grand narratives that have got in the way which prevent us from believing. But we do know when we find ourselves identifying with what happens to Mustafa and the truth that it communicates. Pre-Columbian Texas is the unexpected third space; but we still recognise it. It is a deCentred space from which we can see who we all are. But we need to recognise it as a normal, and in effect *permanent* space.

2   DeCentred threads resist the expected

In this chapter, we build on what we learnt in Chapter 1 about what is common about how we can find deCentred threads in uncomfortable third spaces in both distant and near settings. In all three events in Chapter 1 there was an acute unexpectedness in this process – Kati finding threads even without shared language and background, Matt finding threads only as a result of seriously unseating his thinking-as-normal, and the threads in pre-Colombian Texas defying all expectation and being indigestible within the established neoliberal order. Connected with this is the disturbing of the common notion of cultural integration. In none of these accounts did threads depend upon people being 'the same' as each other. This is particularly noted in Matt's encounter with the woman on the train, where the thread could only be forged when it was revealed as an essentialist block to believe that she 'might be not well-socialised into living here because she only mixed with her own people and was therefore isolated and culturally confused'.

We therefore begin the chapter with the critique of the notion of integration because it underpins the Centre grand narrative of how cultural newcomers should arrive and engage, and somehow needs to be cleared away before we can look at the more unexpected ways that deCentred threads can be forged between all of us wherever we are or 'come from'.

The problem with 'integration'

Integration is often thought to be at the core of what is imagined to be 'success' in intercultural travel. Integration is however a highly contested term that can mean different things to different people. On one level it can mean simply getting along with a particular cultural environment in a way that provides a sense of well-being. However, even that might be problematic because different parties within that environment might have different requirements for what that means.

From a Centre-deCentred perspective, we perceive integration to be a Centre force when it implies a functional belonging to a bounded homogenous cultural whole. This framing is of integration as positivist and essentialist, derived from a notion of travel from one bounded large culture to another. Because the two large cultures are considered to be essentially different, to 'succeed' in the 'target culture' requires acquiring behaviour that integrates with its features. The notion of 'target' emphasises the monodirectional nature of this approach – moving irrevocably towards a single location, with arriving at, engaging with, joining and learning the 'new culture' as the ultimate objective. This Centre view also gives the false impressions of consensus regarding dominant and persistent yet fallacious ideas such as the simplistic capturing of national language and culture in the constructed, culturally idealised person of the 'native speaker' (Holliday 2018b). The Centre perception of a homogenous order is presented in Durkheim's structural-functional sociology. His example of suicide as deviance from the social norms of a functional society 'varies inversely with the degree of integration of the social groups of which the individual forms a part' (1952: 209).

Ambivalence about this Centre view was revealed in a recent conference presentation that reported the experiences of people who travelled from one European country to another to work as assistant teachers of 'their language'. The findings of the study noted that they had not succeeded in making friends and generally mixing with members of the 'target culture'. This was represented as evidence of the lack of success of the intercultural exchange programme in which they were taking part. This equating of intercultural success with joining and making friends is a common theme in study abroad research, where there is a sense of dismay when international students tend to mix with their compatriots and that home students are reluctant to make friends with them (e.g. Osmond & Roed 2009).

However, there was a heated discussion among conference delegates in the room at the end of the presentation. Half the audience felt strongly that making local friends and joining their local groups was far too much to expect of the teachers, that it was quite natural for them to socialise with their own compatriot community, and that this was not a sign of 'failure' in intercultural integration. What we also need to consider here is that all populations are made up of diverse groups of people and that 'local' does not exclude people 'like' the people who travel there – where we are all hybrid, as discussed in Chapter 1. We all, wherever we go, make choices about with whom we wish to associate. Certainly, venturing out of the particular social groups to which we are used might enable us to expand our consciousness of who we and others are, but this should be to search for the deCentred and hybrid in all of us rather than to learn a particular cultural norm.

When they encounter the Centre view of integration, cultural travellers may wish to resist by taking on a deCentred position. An expression of deCentred resistance is in the following statement from Angela Davis about the associated concept of inclusion:

> If we stand up against racism, we want much more than 'inclusion'. 'Inclusion' is not enough. 'Diversity' is not enough and as a matter of fact we do not wish to be 'included' in a racist society.
>
> (2017)

Being 'included' not only does not recognise who she is but is aggressively meaningless when the concept implies racial preference. What might be considered the extreme case of racism cannot be detached from any circumstance where a newcomer is expected to be culturally 'like' the people already there, and where 'culture' is considered to be just a 'nice' way of talking about 'race' (e.g. Hervik 2013). A similar sentiment is expressed with regard to another associated concept of 'assimilation' by Kumaravadivelu:

> The proponents of cultural assimilation would expect me to adopt the behaviours, values, beliefs, and lifestyles of the dominant cultural community and become absorbed in it, losing my own in the process … to have metamorphosed into a somebody with a totally different cultural persona.
>
> (2007: 5)

'Assimilation' perhaps better carries the force, implicit in 'integration' and 'assimilation', of submitting to a Centre that does not recognise the importance of the 'cultural persona' that we bring with us. This resonates with the concepts of 'cultural loss' or 'gain' also implicit in the essentialist, bounded, homogenous large culture idea, where one is expected to be one thing or another – like the polarised 'with us or against us'. The resistance to this sense of polarised identity is seen in the response of the postgraduate student abroad to her landlady who says that she will never become a member of 'our culture' by saying 'I already have a culture' (Amadasi & Holliday 2018). We comment here that she is not being essentialist by pitting her own culture against an incompatible one she found around her, but is rather claiming that she does not need to conform, to assimilate because she can still be herself on her own terms.

This chapter therefore focuses on engaging with deCentred narratives that cultural travellers bring with them, which may not conform to the established Centre narratives of the place at which they are arriving, but which nevertheless contribute richness and enhanced human awareness to that place. These deCentred narratives may come from unexpected places; an overriding principle is that they, and the cultural travellers that bring them, are good for all of us because they shake us out of established thinking. Instead of looking at how cultural travellers can integrate, we therefore focus on combating the prejudice and exclusion that is implicit in the discourse of integration. This does not however imply a cultural relativism in which any passing or established cultural reality is allowed to inhibit human rights.

Working with children as expert agents of culture and identity

This Centre-deCentred tension, around integration and also other issues, becomes evident in those situations where the established institutional discourse, based on and reproducing an essentialist grand narrative, face a series of social events which create a crack in the system. By disturbing the flow of the institutional narrative, this crack causes the system to rebalance as it responds to the irruption brought about by the changes. On the one hand, this will force the dominant essentialist discourse into greater visibility. On the other hand, new narratives will develop. Some of them will conform to and strengthen the Centre; but some will take on a new, deCentred perspective.

This happened in a primary school where Sara was teaching Italian as a second language. Some of the pupils who were supposed to attend a workshop a few weeks before school started, to warm up their Italian, did not show up. The school had not been warned of this absence. All these children had a family migration history; and most of them were still abroad, having spent the whole summer period at their parents' countries of departure. Sara began to hear comments that started to populate conversations between the teachers. They expressed worries about these long stays abroad; and most of them seemed to fear that their pupils might experience a loss in their cultural and language knowledge due to these long-term trips to their birth countries. The teachers' comments represented and revealed the essentialist grand narrative of the institution, that the travel of the children with migration backgrounds back to the non-Western locations of their parents damaged their integration into 'Italian culture'. This is in sharp contrast to travel to Western locations, which is thought of as 'educational tourism'.

It was as a result of witnessing this narrative of child disorientation and displacement that Sara decided to research the children's perceptions of these trips when she got her PhD position a few months later. She sensed that there would be a very different narrative coming from the children – that this travel enhanced rather than damaged their cultural identity. The issue was not that the children could never be disoriented or feel displaced, but that it should not be assumed that they would *always* be because of their cultural background.

In this chapter we will focus on the first part of the research, in one of the primary schools that constituted the wider project, with children with migration backgrounds aged seven to ten. Through interactions with the children within a series of workshops, Sara investigated their active participation in being expert agents of culture and identity. What we are particularly interested in, however, is not only children's agency, but how the involvement of the researcher with them opens further opportunities for self-expression and the possibilities for deCentring narratives and threads to arise, though not always as might be expected.

To get a fuller picture of the different elements of the small culture formation on the go that took place between Sara and the children, it is important to take their developing relationship right back to Sara's initial entry into the field – the early stage in the ethnographic process in which the researcher looks around to see what it is going on to gradually determine how to proceed. This will show how Sara herself, as the participant researcher, and the children, even at the early stage of noticing each other, enter into a negotiation of narratives and meanings which is itself evidence of the children's agentive ownership of the intercultural, even though their own knowledge of this might remain tacit.

Research events as expert exchange

The fact of agency is laced throughout the narratives, which people *choose*, and the small cultures, which they *form* on the go, as a matrix of social action. The research event is itself a site where agency is enacted through choices within a 'socially constituted' set of interactions in which participants can 'make a difference' or 'could have acted differently' (Barker & Galasiński 2001; Giddens 1984). This is more obviously the case with the interactions observed in the workshops that Sara set up with the children to collect and promote their expression of narratives about the countries they had visited. However, it is also the case where the researcher spends time in the research site to see what is going on or to develop relationships. Agency here implies not a personal psychological or behavioural disposition, but a space – with its own constraints – where all of us make choices. In the research event these choices are derived from expertise in intercultural negotiation and sense-making. While the researchers who set up the event are expert in academic research and discussion of intercultural issues, the people they research are expert in their own intercultural trajectory experience. This is a major factor in why we chose to research them.

Belief in the agency and expertise of the people being researched strengthens the licence of the researchers to intervene where it is felt that this expertise can contribute to the creation of a third space. In this third space, new positionings and alternative narratives linked to these positionings can emerge. Therefore, in this particular case, being a teenager or a child with a migration background is no longer considered to be an institutionalised disadvantaged position that has to be corrected, but becomes one positioning possibility amongst others. The agenda that researchers of the intercultural bring to the research event is therefore a narrative one – to reveal and create new stories about the intercultural expertise that those being interacted with bring with them as they engage with small culture formation on the go. However, where established institutional discourses are dominant and no space for a deCentred position is allowed, new meanings and narratives around the experiences of personal and cultural journeys might just be hidden, or relegated to problematic views.

Initial researcher reflection (Sara's voice)

My work with the children in the primary school had several phases. The first comprised a period of five months of preliminary ethnographic observation in the Italian as a second language classes which I attended with the children. This phase was not only to let the children familiarise with me and my presence, but also to negotiate the second phase of the project with their teachers. This first stage thus represented a progressive field-access strategy, the purpose of which was not only 'the accomplishment of the research plan but also the securing and setting up of an appropriate situational context for the research process' (Wolff 2004: 202).

The entire process of collecting consent forms was an important part of this familiarisation. Through the help of mediators in the school, forms were distributed both in Italian and in the other two main languages of children's families, to fully inform them about the research, its topic, data collection methods and future use. Signatures from both parents were required, and their children were guaranteed anonymity and the use of pseudonyms. A similar consent form was distributed also to the children. While this form did not have any legal value, it had an ethical relevance: to make the children fully aware of their engagement in the research and give them the possibility to withdraw whenever they felt the need to do so.

These negotiations were instrumental for how the relationship with the children slowly took shape. They were rich with reflections about the several domains that research in an institutional setting implies. I had to consider carefully my relationship with the children, to build trust with them, and trying not to be considered a teacher. For example, I asked them several times to call me by name, Sara, rather than 'prof' or 'maestra'.[1] But at the same time, I also had to pay attention to the relationship with the teachers, as gatekeepers of the school institution, to gain also their trust and negotiate better my space of intervention with the children. While my interactions with the children were limited, as I only attended their classes silently, I was able to focus on small details like glimpses, smiles and those few moments in which teachers left the classes and asked me to stay alone with them. In my research diary, I wrote:

> I don't intervene, and I don't speak. So far, I limit myself to observe them and exchanging gazes with them. Sometimes, if they look at me insistently, I only stay there looking at them, without doing anything else. Other times I smile a bit. But not too much. Differently from other situations in which I worked with young people, now I feel the need to define my presence differently from that of a teacher, but at the same time to build a respectful relationship …
>
> In this phase I am thinking about my days in Senegal. Knowing people in those days was exactly like now, a slow process, made out of starting, mutual and at distance observation. In this way, I managed to create with some of them a relationship of trust. I hope not to be mistaken if I think that, in the end, all social relations, and mainly those that are born in a research context, need to be envisaging a phase in which I let the community who is hosting me scrutinise me, murmur about me. A phase in which they wonder about me and my presence amongst them.
>
> I feel the need to be known with extreme naturalness, without the will to give them a defined and precise idea of me. The quicker I define myself, the quicker they will define themselves in my eyes, and the relationship between us will be defined. Wouldn't this create even more artificiality in my work?

The reference in the field diary to my fieldwork in Senegal, which took place in 2009, reveals the aspect of small culture formation on the go where we make connections backward and forward in our personal cultural trajectories to help make sense of the present, and to see the relevance of past cultural encounters for the present. Such interconnections do not have to be with similar geographical places. The fieldwork in Senegal was the most recent and significant fieldwork I conducted at that time before the research

---

1 These are the ways students address teachers in Italian first grade secondary and primary school.

I was conducting when these notes were taken. Referring to it was therefore part of an ongoing process of personal and professional work to sharpen my criticality and reflexivity about the intercultural and to construct my own narratives about it. There is a reflexivity which becomes particularly urgent to explain and clarify in those situations that bring you to call into question the filters through which you observe and make sense of what is around you, as it was for me in my experience in Senegal.

Setting up the workshops

In the second phase, I presented the project to them in a 30-minute meeting. I told them that I was interested in working with them because they travelled to Italy from other countries and *vice versa*. I gave them one camera each to take pictures of moments, objects and people through which they could describe their relationships with these countries, and to provide them with material to bring to the workshops.

This could be considered an intermediate phase, between the initial looking around and the workshops, in which pupils started to know me and my aims. Now they knew that I was interested in their experience of travel. They started to move closer to me and to share their stories, perhaps on the basis of a faint idea they were constructing about me and my work, although I still had not asked them more than a few questions. Some of them had already experienced one or more temporary returns to their parents' countries of origin. The children's families mainly came from Pakistan and India; but there were also children who were born in Macedonia, Morocco and Senegal. It then happened that some of the girls came to me and started to speak about their items of clothing, which they had bought in Pakistan or India, or they told me about their grandparents that they had left there. Some of them asked me if they could show me the country where they were born on the map. On some occasions, a small question from me, concerning clothing or other details, was taken by the children as an opportunity to begin a narrative about themselves and their families and thus as an occasion to let me know something more about them. An example of this is in the following entry from my research diary:

> This morning the teacher asks me to help Shahlyla and Arham with their homework. Shahlyla wears a Salwar Kameez that I had never seen on her. It is beautiful. So, I tell her that it is lovely. She tells me that it was given her by her grandma, who brought it from Pakistan when she came to visit some years ago. But it was too big for her at that time; so, she had to wait to grow up a bit before wearing it. Then I ask her if her grandma is still here. And she answers, 'Noooo she went back to

Pakistan!'. Working with them is nice: they are brother and sister and she keeps interrupting him while talking to me. I have always seen her very silent, but now, with me, she is prepared to share her thoughts. At the end of the hour, also Yalina arrives. She has Bordeaux nail polish and I tell her that it looks very nice. Then Shahlyla shows me her hand, where there are still visible drawings. I ask her what these drawings are and they both answer me with maybe an Urdu word[2] that I can't understand. They repeat the word several times to let me learn it. They tell me these drawings are painted to make the hand more beautiful. I ask them who the one who painted them is. And they reply that it was the mom, but the aunt too.

As in the workshops that eventually took place, during the introductory meetings, considerable positioning took place between me and the children. The following sequence is taken from the 30-minute introductory meeting with Parmesh, Umar, Qasim, Ajeet and Saeed:

Sequence 1

1. Sara: well, I was asking (.) who remembers the reason why I'm here? ((all rise hands up)) Everybody- ((addressing Parmesh)) go ahead
2. Parmesh: eh?
3. Sara: tell me Parmesh, what you were saying (.) why am I here (.) because?
4. Parmesh: because: because you make work children (0.2) children
5. Sara: yes I'm a researcher- Who knows what a researcher is?
6. Umar: ah mm like err they look for things
7. Sara: they look for things and they study things ((Qasim rises his hand up to say something)) tell me
8. Qasim: and you make work foreign children?
9. Sara: and I work with children (.) that have err travelled let's say (0.2) that have travelled- why? Because I'm interested in know-ing (.) firstly because few researchers work with children (0.3) and I'm interested a lot in knowing what children think ((teacher's interruption))
    […]
10. Sara: well err mm (.) well the researcher is a person who studies and looks for things (.) some researchers study mountains and eh

---

2 Here children are talking about *mehndi*, a temporary henna tattoo.

11. Parmesh: Alps Apennines (those things)
12. Sara: yes (.) there are people who study: animals there people who study seas fish (0.3) I can't see Saeed in this way- ((teacher's interruption))

In the first part of this extract, Qasim positions himself, and in doing this, he also positions the whole group: in turn 8, Qasim asks me whether I normally work with *foreign children*. As a response, I do not confirm this positioning and reply to Qasim by introducing a new one: that I work with children *who travelled* (turn 9). By purposefully not defining the nature of the travel and by not referring thus to 'migration' movement, my aim is to avoid introducing information that might affect the development of the interaction and its content.

My intention here is to focus on the act of travelling *per se*, as an experience. This is of course difficult because I am trying to get the children to discuss beyond framing and categories that might have been common and imposed on them inside school regarding their travel. It is by introducing new positionings related to the children, which are alternative to the set of established positionings the educational system has given them, that I tried to stimulate, together with the children, the production of alternative narratives (Baraldi 2014a).

It is thus by deconstructing existing dominant, Centre narratives that alternative, deCentred narratives can be produced, paying close attention to avoiding essentialist blocks, as can be seen in the next extract from the same meeting. Here we also see the class teacher taking part. Although the teachers had to be present during all the workshops for security reasons, they were not supposed to participate in the discussion, but sometimes did. A further reason for including this particular extract is that the teachers present the conflict between the emerging deCentring narrative of the children and the Centre grand narrative of the institution. This can be seen in the second sequence:

Sequence 2

1. Sara: I study people who have travelled instead (.) because I want to know- I want to know what they say about those places which they travelled to- those countries they visited and the journeys they had and most of all- but I study this from the perspective of what children think because few people ask- few researchers ask children what they think- or to young people (.) and I want to ask young people who travelled instead (.) and since you have travelled and you are young and you saw countries I haven't seen- you came from- from India from Pakistan

2. Ajeet: India!
3. Sara: from India
4. Qasim: Pakistan!
5. Sara: ((laughs)) and then I would like you to tell me a bit how- how it was the journeys you had, how is your parents' country if you went back there and to do this we will (0.2) we will play like
6. Saeed: you- ((chaos))
7. Parmesh: to me I don't remember ((laughs))
8. Sara: what is that you don't remember?
9. Teacher: *I don't* remember is the way to say it <I don't remember>
10. Parmesh: the journey
11. Sara: you don't remember the journey? Never mind you will tell me whatever you want to tell me
12. Teacher: I can hear a pot of beans[3]
13. Saeed: you are a bean! ((teacher speaking))
14. Sara: fine Parmesh was telling me that he can't remember the journey and does anyone remember the journey?
15. Qasim: me! I remember very well!
16. Sara: you remember- good there will be someone who does not remember and someone who does then- but we will talk and we will play and we use a story that is the story of a child who travelled a lot and I will tell you this story and you can tell me if you like it- I like this story very much but I share it with you because I'd like to know what you think about it (.) if you like it or not

My positioning is introduced again (turn 5), when, as response to two children's statements concerning their specific origin (turns 2 and 4), I bring the attention back to children as expert travellers and children as experts of places I do not know. This positioning suggestion generates two different reactions: on the one hand, in turn 7, Parmesh intervenes to say that he cannot remember anything about the journey, thus mildly rejecting the positioning I have suggested; on the other hand, Qasim accepts it by claiming to remember it 'very well'.

The teacher's interventions in turns 9 and 12 are very different from mine in that they are more evaluative than negotiatory. The roles of the teacher and the students seem fixed, and reproduce the school structure. Her Centring role thus serves to emphasise the difference from the deCentring nature of the facilitation in the other turns in the extract, which focuses

---

3 'I can hear a pot of beans' is an expression used by teachers to warn pupils that they are making a constant background noise – like a bubbling pot in which beans are being cooked.

not only on the content but also on the form of communication, with the aim of breaking the narratives anchored to structured roles and of promoting self-expression. The aim of turn 11, for example, is to go beyond this pedagogical form ('you don't remember the journey? *Never mind you will tell me whatever you want to tell me*') and introduce the possibility of self-expression that is free from a potentially blocking idea of educational evaluation and performance.

Being experts and expert travellers here thus represents a positioning which is ascribed from me to the participants. However, this positioning is not always accepted and taken up. There are a number of reasons why this might be the case, including the possibility of being taken in by the Centre narrative of the institution, which ignores the expertise of the cultural traveller. It is also possible that their sense of agency rejects what might be perceived by them as interference from any other party. Whatever the reason, their resistance to positioning is itself an act of expert agency.

First meeting

Once the workshops began, they each comprised a number of encounters. The following sequence is from the first one with Paolo, Munirah, Andrea (who does not appear in the extract), Mor, Loveleen, Nimrit, Said and Hamed. In this particular group, although they were all attending the Italian as second language class, they had very different levels of knowledge of Italian: some of them were born in Italy, others arrived while still very young and other participants arrived less than a year before the research work started.

Inside this group some children experienced meaningful journey experiences: although they were both born in Italy, Said spent all his summer holidays in Morocco while Mor lived in Senegal for some years after and then came back to Italy to begin primary school; Paolo and Andrea were also born in Italy, but they went to Macedonia several times to meet some relatives there; Nimrit had just come back from a journey to India that lasted some weeks; and, finally, Loveleen suddenly left during that same school year, between the second and the third research encounter. Loveleen's departure was exactly one of those departures that worried the teachers most because it happened in an unexpected way, with no warning from the family, and the destination was not known, though there were rumours in the school that she travelled back to India.

Because I had already had a meeting with this group to present the workshops, in the first turns of this conversation I am asking the children if they remembered the reason why I was there working with them. Paolo has just intervened in a playful way to claim that I might be an international spy, and by doing so, he seems to be testing the level of playfulness of the meeting we are going to have together.

Sequence 3

1. Sara: fine, I'm not a spy (.) Who knows what I'm doing? Who remembers it?
2. Said: you do-
3. Paolo: wait waitwa- (.) the University!
4. Sara: the University- go ahead Mor tell me please
5. Mor: because you want to know about us foreigner children if the language is hard
6. Sara: well let's say that I want to know about you children (.) because you travelled a lot, this is the reason
7. Paolo: I didn't
8. Sara: mm are you sure?
9. Paolo: yes
10. Sara: but you told me you went to Macedonia few times
11. Paolo: two I think
12. Said: I went to Morocco
13. Sara: you went to Morocco (.) but now actually we are here to talk and tell us things
14. Said: and in France
15. Sara: and also in France?
16. Nimrit: I have nothing to te- to tell
17. Said: yes but I don't remember anything because I was very young
18. Sara: I start to tell you something then, fine? Is it better? Well here there are- who knows- do you know their names?
19. Paolo: no
20. Sara: let's start with a presentation

As with Parmesh at the beginning of sequence 1, Mor positions himself by ascribing being *foreign* to himself and the group ('because you want to know about us *foreign children*'): by rejecting this positioning, I propose to them a different interpretation of their hypothetical 'foreignness', stressing their competence as travellers rather than their belonging to a particular cultural location. This deCentred positioning as experts of travel ('well let's say that I want to know about you children because you travelled a lot') is thus offered to them as a counter to the Centre positioning that has been imposed upon them – the grand narrative of cultural incompetence resulting from discordant cultural diversity and confusion. Moreover, this new deCentred positioning emphasises meanings that are under construction through personal experience, which opposes the *a priori* negative Centre connotations.

As in sequence 1, this deCentred positioning through meanings under construction generates different reactions. In turn 7, Paolo rejects the positioning I suggested when I questioned his response in turn 9, and he confirms his response by replying 'yes'. Said instead confirms the assignment of my positioning by mentioning two of his journeys, to Morocco and France (turn 12 and 14). However, when Nimrit refuses this position in turn 16, this generates a change also in Said's positioning, who now backtracks, and denies it by claiming not to remember anything because he was too young (turn 17). As with Parmesh in sequence 1, the narrative of 'not remembering' allows participants to reject in a mitigated form a positioning and the responsibilities deriving from it (for instance, here, the request to tell the group about personal experience and details of a journey).

The intertwined nature of identity construction

This complex intertwining of positionings does not only represent an example of narrative identity construction, but it is an opportunity to reflect on small culture formation which takes place in any research context. These interactions are in fact empirical examples of the heterogeneous ways in which participants choose to approach a new interactional and social event and the generation of relationships to which the workshop is contributing. There could be many implications arising from the conversational extracts in this chapter as, in our view, they inspire reflections about the caution and attention with which children face a relationship with someone who is somehow new to them and who is proposing to them to take part in an activity which is different from ordinary classes, where roles and expectations are not fully disclosed to them and still in a process of becoming.

As researchers, we cannot ignore the fact that these dynamics are there whenever we are collecting data; and that the people we are interacting with have expectations about the encounter with us as we have with them, and as we all have when we are approaching a social event. Goffman can be helpful here:

> Information about the individual helps to define the situation, enabling others to know in advance what he will expect of them and what they may expect of him. Informed in these ways, the others will know how best to act in order to call forth a desired response from him. ... When an individual appears before others his actions will influence the definition of the situation which they come to have.
>
> (1959: 1)

If interpreted according to Goffman, these conversation extracts show how the children are carefully evaluating the situation and carrying out a preliminary, ongoing observation of expectations and balances amongst all the participants. We could also say that what is realised here is a political dynamic, where the children seem to explore and test their relationship with the researcher and the power forces at stake. This underpins what we earlier refer to as emergent positionings.

Moreover, we should not ignore that Sara tried during her interventions to apply a different communication system from that normally found in educational settings, by adopting with participants the technique of *facilitation*. By allowing the reworking of initial narratives through the dialogue together with the children (Baraldi 2014a), we claim that facilitation puts into action a process which aims to produce new deCentred narratives. But to do so, it needs to be noted that facilitation only works if it *is* deCentred. In these specific conversations for example, what is valued through this technique is the children's self-expression: any form of educational evaluation is suspended, and the aim is to promote active participation, sustaining the possibility of coexistence between different opinions. Since facilitation recognises participants as persons, dissolving diversities created by differential roles, what is expected is the expression of personal perspectives which implies that the event is characterised by a higher level of unpredictability.

Thinking back to the discussion of Lalami's *The Moor's Account* in Chapter 1, the Spanish colonial authorities in Mexico wanted to construct, as an 'excuse' to extend their empire, 'the facilitation' of 'civilising' Christianity. It is therefore necessary to make sure that facilitation values unexpected narratives to the extent that they *disturb* the Centre and its consolidated narratives – just as 'the Moor's' *real* account of the already civilised people he has encountered *disturbs* the colonial authorities.

The extracts from conversations with the children in this chapter are therefore relevant, in our opinion, to understanding not only Centre *cultural presuppositions* (Gumperz 1992), which often guide communication, not only during established research encounters, but also during those related to educational communication in which children are involved on a daily basis. The dynamic of attribution of positionings permits us to see these presuppositions in interactions and to make them visible. On one side, children tend to position themselves in the category of 'foreign children'. This implies a set of Centre expectations imposed upon them related to learning processes and educational rules that need to be followed. It is relevant to notice for example that this positioning that children are seduced by is legitimised by the learning of Italian as a second language. Their need for special assistance with language and literacy thus becomes a main feature through which their identities are observed and qualified as a process of Othering inside the school, with the risk that – in school environments as well as in academic studies – they are subjected to the Centre labelling of '"disadvantaged" groups' (Wallace 2011: 102).

This point resonates the notion of the West as steward discourse, introduced in Chapter 1, that everything of value that can be learnt must come from the West. Examples of this are with secondary school and university students in China (Gong & Holliday 2013), the United Arab Emirates (Yamchi 2015) and Kuwait (Kamal 2015). As with the children in Sara's study, different forms of intervention need to be employed in the above studies to shake the students out of the deeply established Centre structures to which they have become used.

The deCentred positioning proposed in this chapter, in which children are proposed to be expert travellers, embodies a third space in which Centre rights in knowledge production are overturned. In this third space, Italian adult teachers no longer have a monopoly of knowledge and expertise from which the children are there to learn. Instead, it is possible to observe an equal, active participation amongst all children.

A critical cosmopolitan, deCentred discourse of culture

The analysis of the conversations that took place while setting up and during the workshops so far demonstrates how these children with migration backgrounds support the alternative, critical cosmopolitan discourse of culture by showing that they are expert intercultural travellers and active agents of culture and identity, and not, as their teachers think, suffering from cultural displacement and language loss.

Although on some occasions they might seem to resist Sara's positioning of them as expert travellers, this should not be read as alignment with the Centre essentialist discourse of their teachers. This is, rather, evidence that *by* moving inside a framework of contradictory, ambivalent narratives, the children *choose* to adopt these narratives in order to interactionally perform and display a certain identity. This is in contrast to the teachers' belief that they are not able to understand what is happening concerning these journeys, and that they are overpowered by what the teachers construct as 'two or more contradictory homogenous cultures'.

We might therefore say that they apply these contradictory narratives as identity tools to construct meanings about their travel and identity in the same way as any adult would. Moreover, these meanings are skilfully negotiated with others. Therefore, the children are *not* living their experiences of travel as passive receivers. Instead, they present the sorts of ambivalences, contradictory and even instrumental opinions and experiences that make them fully social actors. In this sense, they are indicating *threads* of experience that should resonate with any adult from any background. One might then ask why, if this is the case, their teachers do not recognise this. We wish to argue that this is because their teachers' vision is inhibited by the Centre narrative of the school institution.

The next sequence shows this well:

Sequence 4

1. Mor: miss, I am sad a bit sad because when I will go- when I will go- I will go to Paris after next year that is coming- my mum said that I will go to Paris and I will stay there until I am 17 years old so that I don't see my mat- mates
2. Sara: so (.) so she said that you will stay there until you are 17 years old?
3. Mor: err
4. Sara: and what is the reason?
5. Hamed: seventeen years old?
6. Sara: until you are sevent- and why?
7. Mor: err because my da- my father is there
8. Sara: ah your dad is in Paris?
9. Mor: yes
10. Sara: and you don't want to go there?
11. Mor: I want to go there but the thing is my friends!

In this sequence, Mor expresses deeply and clearly his personal feelings concerning the future possibility of moving to France. The ambivalence he describes and the contradictory feelings he expresses is a thread that many of us might have experienced once in our lives. Feeling an attachment to more places where important relationships take place is not just something that a child can experience. Moreover, the possibility of self-expression, free from forms of evaluation which this third space gives to the children, encourages Mor to show the meaningful awareness he has about the dynamics of travel. By showing his emotions and fears, he is making an important choice which does not reveal a passivity towards social events, but rather a certain strength in recognising, naming and sharing ('Maestra, I am sad a bit sad') these emotions with a group of other people where there are both children and an adult present.

In contrast to this, in the final sequence, we see the children taking up clearly opposite positions about their cultural identity. On these occasions, differently from the deCentred narrative of ambivalence adopted by Mor in sequence 4, the children sustain their identity positioning, also through Centre essentialist narratives:

Sequence 5

1. Sara: when you go- when you went to India what was it like with friends you left there?
2. Nimrit: awful ((all become silent))
3. Sara: awful? Why?
4. Nimrit: because there- because in Italy there are many friends and we have fun and there, they don't know anything to play
5. Sara: ah and so you didn't know who to play with?
6. Nimrit: they didn't even know how to play
7. Sara: they didn't know how to play? ((she nods)) No? So, what did you do?
8. Loveleen: to me not- they didn't know those games they played in India so they taught me
9. Sara: those games you didn't know did they teach you?
10. Loveleen: yes
11. Sara: and what about you Nimrit? Did you ask them to teach you those games or didn't you play?
12. Nimrit: I didn't play

Thus, Nimrit openly declares her distance from India and her belonging to Italy 'because there- because in Italy there are many friends and we have fun and there, they don't know anything to play'. As with Mor, in sequence 4, Nimrit is here making her choice of self-expression. All these positional choices should not be interpreted as mere innate features of each participant. Instead, they have to be observed as the result of complex interactional dynamics inside the group and the result of children's choices in relation to Centre structures or deCentring opportunities that they feel around them. We are thus not evaluating whether the children are more or less essentialist than adults. Instead, we would like to distance ourselves from a binary interpretation of participants reactions – that multiple cultural influences are negative to them versus multiple cultural influences are positive to them – by proposing an interpretation which looks at the coexistence of multiple, overlapping and even contradictory possibilities. This permits us to avoid an evaluative approach and to focus on *how* blocking narratives are generated in the interaction and *what* effects these have on the reproduction of a Centre perspective.

Regarding their ability to use the Italian language, this is what the children are employing perfectly adequately as they express these ambivalences. It is about how people go about negotiating rather than what they actually come out with at the end. What is evident in a number of the conversations with the children in this chapter is that even when they do not conform to the positioning that Sara proposes to them, they show more than she expected. Sara is trying to construct with them meanings that bring out their abilities to manage the complexity of multiple identities. Sometimes they resist this; and in so doing they display a creative criticality which is far more than she expected. It is not therefore the particular content of small culture formation on the go that provides evidence for interculturality, but the process of culture formation through which it takes place.

Searching for hidden spaces

In this chapter we have shown how we researchers, in our interactions with the people we encounter in our research, attempted to put aside Centre essentialist blocks and to search for deCentred non-essentialist threads. In Sara's interactions with the children in the Italian school, she is conscious of having to work hard to overcome particular established blocks of which she was already aware because she witnessed how they were embedded in the Centre institutional structures of schooling. These blocks concern the structures of pedagogy and educational evaluation and performance. They are also evident in the teachers' narrative which claims that the children are confused by their experience of intercultural travel and that this confusion inhibits them from being socialised into their image of Italian culture. These blocking narratives are then contrasted with thread narratives, constructed through the introduction of a new set of positionings, in which the children emerge as expert travellers. It is the personal cultural trajectories that emerge within these thread narratives that we can all relate to across structural restrictions. They are the institutional blocks, implicit in the 'ideological and social reproduction' function of the school that (Canagarajah 2004: 119–120) argues 'prevents students from negotiating favourable identities'. He suggests that researchers can as a result find it hard to see anything but the 'unitary identities (shaped by notions of deficiency, inferiority and disadvantage) conferred on them by the dominant discourse' (117); and that we must therefore search for the 'hidden spaces' where students 'negotiate' other identities (118).

It is for this reason that we feel that researching the intercultural needs to liberate itself from common educational and transformative narratives of intercultural learning and competence that lock our search for making sense of the intercultural into narratives of achievement and change within institutional mechanisms for 'success' in negotiating and crossing imagined national cultural boundaries.

3   Centred threads become blocks

Following the theme of unexpectedness referred to at the beginning of Chapter 2, what is particularly important is that the threads that Sara initially thought that she was extending, through the positioning that she believed would be meaningful to them, were rejected by some children. Threads are therefore in themselves not straightforward and may appear to be threads when in fact they are blocks. While for Sara they were genuine threads, they may not be received as such by the people she is interacting with. It must not however be forgotten that even though they did not apparently succeed in the short-term, the overall effect of finding the unexpected in the children was actually a thread. In this chapter, therefore, we explore the difficult and often unexpected dynamics of blocks and threads inside a broader interactional framework that will reveal the danger of threads remaining Centred and thus becoming blocks. We hope to show how apparent threads intertwine with blocks and can often defy rather than build deCentred positionings, narratives and third space.

Choosing to find threads

The discussion of blocks and threads has been referred to in a number of places (Holliday 2016b: 322,2018c). The following are extracts from Adrian's original blog on the subject.[1] We present these extracts here because they indicate the trajectory of sense-making in developing the concept. The blog begins with the nature of the differences between us which are undeniable:

> There is no question at all that we are culturally different to each other because of the way we are brought up in different nation states. So much of who we are and what we think is influenced by educational,

---

1 http://adrianholliday.com/talking-about-cultural-difference-blocks-and-threads/. These extracts are also used in Holliday (2016b: 320, 322; 2018c: 45).

political, economic and media systems that are often specific to national structures and policies. Then there are life-defining resources to do with climate, physical geography, and agriculture, some of which can also be influenced or even determined by national and geo-politics.

However, the next statement is one of personal assertion against this state of affairs. Perhaps this is made possible by the observation in the first statement that there is a politics and a negotiable softness, in the reference to media and education, within the structures of difference.

> These things are not however the issue. It is what happens next that is important – what we do with and how we think about and frame these backgrounds.

The Centre forces that divide us are already there, as a matter of fact, but it is what we do about them that is at stake. This invokes the element of social action and agency seen amongst the school children in Chapter 2. It is also seen in the choices Sara makes to investigate the possibility that the teachers' narrative, constructing children as always culturally confused because of their migration backgrounds, is the result of questionable Centre structures. Having the agency and the choice in 'what we do next' cannot always mean physical action. There will be all types of Centre political and economic constraints. Just thinking in these terms will itself be important. Simply thinking critically about how the people have been constructed for us as 'the Other' by education and the media is itself a significant form of social action and agency. First of all, it is important to imagine what the blocks are:

> I find it helpful here to distinguish between blocks and threads as alternative ways of thinking and talking about cultural difference. This exchange is an example of blocks – asking questions and getting answers that encourage us to think about cultural barriers:

>> 'How do people in your culture behave at mealtimes?' 'The whole family arrives on time and eats together; and show their appreciation of the person who has prepared the meal, who is normally the mother.' 'Oh, interesting. That's a bit different to my culture and others I have been to, where the whole thing is less formal and organised. But we can certainly learn from each other in this respect.'

> There is some sharing here; but it doesn't really get beyond an 'us'-'them' concept of 'my culture' and 'your culture'. The barriers remain up. It stops dangerously at tolerance.

Of course, the reference to Centre 'barriers' is to what we and others construct. Perhaps they are not real barriers to be crossed, but, instead, imaginations of barriers to be dissolved. The notion of tolerance is problematic because it grows from 'us' trying to reduce our prejudices for 'them' over there in their separate national cultures. Indeed, the notion of tolerance seems to require and enforce 'this culture', 'this group', 'that culture', 'that group' demarcations. As a British Asian woman states about how she is received in British society: 'But tolerance is such a patronising concept. To be tolerant of someone is to accept them grudgingly. We need to accept diversity as an intrinsic good.' (Sardar 2009: 332). The concept of threads is meant to move much further than tolerance of the Other:

> What I mean by threads is quite different – searching for ways to share experiences – threads of cultural experience that we carry with us but that can resonate with those of others.

And then the element of choice is made clear in this short reconstruction. 'Having to work on this' is perhaps the key phrase:

> When I find myself talking to two people sitting at the next table in a café in Algiers, I have to work on this by looking for cultural threads that might bring us together. Perhaps they are interested in talking to me, and make the first move, because I look foreign, might have rather clumsily looked for a table and been generally uncertain about how to come and sit down in a café like this one in Algiers. However, instead of looking at them as essentially foreign, which would be easy, I have to focus on how they are café sitters like me. So I talk to them about cafés, about how good it is to sit and relax, about the sorts of work that we have, leisure activities, where we have travelled to, what it is like to be away from home, this part of the city and its history, and so on.

Of course, one can never know how completely successful the decision to share experience is. Adrian, the observer, has no idea what is going on in the minds of the people he is talking to. Adrian has not met the Algerians at the next table before and never will again. He does not know what they each feel when they perceive their particular Centre constraints to be. This really is therefore small culture formation on the go at its most transient. But there is enough small culture there to allow communication to happen for a fleeting moment. Adrian remembers at the time of writing that he leant over towards their table, and they leant over from theirs. They were sitting side by side; and they were looking out, he felt, together, beyond the café to the square and the port area beyond. It is also just possible that they were not 'Algerians' at all. This was Adrian's firm concept of who they were that populated his image of the conversation. Perhaps they did not feel that their brief encounter was sufficiently important to go into any depth at all about how they constructed their own identities. Threads are assertive moments of contact making. The full implications might never be clear. For as long as they seem to work, they seem to work.

The next reconstruction in the blog is of a less transient instance of small culture formation on the go because it is with the person assigned to Adrian at the conference he is attending:

> On another occasion I am with a young Chinese man who is taking me in his car to a conference. (It's his job to look after me for the day as a visiting speaker.) Imagining his age and perhaps noticing some young children things on the back seat, I use my recent experience with my daughter and grandchildren to talk to him about childcare, how being a parent impacts on his career and so on.

While he has not met the 'Chinese man' before, Adrian has some background knowledge of what sort of person he might be. He has been to a number of conferences in China at which he has been assigned a number of students or academics to accompany him. He has also known a number of Chinese students about the same age as this man with whom he has had many conversations about their lives and their studies. His daughter, who is his model in the event for childcare, is also a university academic along with a range of younger colleagues who have talked to him about work-life balance – with the knowledge that many young academics like her feel strongly about the Centre neoliberal pressures that pertain to this. At the same time he chooses not to mention the Chinese government one-child policy. The purpose of mentioning all this is to note the nature of background knowledge that Adrian brings to his decision to find threads or experience to share. Thinking back to 'the Algerians' in the café, Adrian also brings what he imagines to be people like them from cultural backgrounds that he imagines might be like theirs – drawing on the resonances across space and time that constitute our intercultural knowledge.

There is a third space of caution and uncertainty implicit in the experiences that give Adrian the courage to choose to draw threads. Intersubjectivity runs throughout these choices. However, the next extract connects this with what we all have to deal with in all our interactions, and that it is learning how to manage them, that might be the route to the content of intercultural education:

> I suppose this is not unlike making conversation a lot of the time. But we do have to work at it – searching for resonances. While cultural

difference is still on the agenda, the effect can be to open up possibilities for sharing and crossing boundaries. This does however mean that the act of talking to people about cultural difference, whether in interviews or in conversation, or in the sort of interpersonal research cultural travellers may engage in, might be something strategic to do – to get to talking and thinking that gets us to new places of understanding about who we are and how we can be together. For the first time, surprisingly, I can see a route here through to a possibility for intercultural training!

The reference to training connects with Adrian's recent publication on the subject (Holliday 2018a), which recommends that intercultural education should focus on awareness of the politics that underlie the narratives, discourses and ideologies that surround the intercultural choices that are available to us. It is recommended there that we can employ the model provided by the sub-discipline of cultural studies in its emphasis, driven by the work of Stuart Hall and Raymond Williams, on a 'radical project' to interrogate the power structures that oppress or alienate the cultural creativity of the individual – '"to rescue education from the influence of the ruling class"' (Blackman 2000b: 62, citing Marx, and Engels), and to bring about '"critical intervention"' with regard to '"race, gender and sexual practice"' (63, citing bell hooks). As discussed with regard to bell hooks in Chapter 1, this is a deCentred intervention, and resonates strongly with the intercultural awareness aims of the IEREST materials for study-abroad university students in Europe (Beaven & Borghetti 2015: 8-14), in which there is a radical project to re-interrogate selves through a reflexive critique of established Centre structures.

The personal political agendas that connect with these larger Centre narratives and which underpin blocking narratives are dealt with in the next of Adrian's blogs on the subject of blocks and threads:[2]

Of course, in our everyday conversations, we move between block and thread ways of talking about cultural difference all the time. The block mode – 'my culture' 'your culture' – is what we have somehow, all of us, grown up with as our default language for talking about culture, probably because of our recent modern histories of cultural nationalism.

So sometimes we do need to reinforce our senses of identity by projecting stories of cultural exclusivity; and we might even believe them

---

2 http://adrianholliday.com/moving-between-blocks-and-threads-sharing-humanity/

for the moment when we are doing this. We might even believe these things about ourselves and the people we want to be associated with most of the time.

The reference to and caution about everyday conversations, as well as everyday Centre structures, will be taken up in the second part of the chapter, where we look in detail at a conversation that arises from a research interview. The next section shows how threads may indeed not be what they seem and that they may in fact feed essentialist blocks.

Dangerous threads: Kati and Eli

It is the unexpected complexity of the threads that Sara is able to explore with the children that begins to show us that it is important not to be simplistic about blocks and threads. Indeed, threads do not always bring people together in a positive way, as blocks also depend on threads. The following blog indicates this with caution:[3]

> We cannot be naïve about the simple value of threads – about pulling threads from our own cultural experience to meet with those of others, and thus to begin crossing cultural boundaries. ... There will clearly be times when this does not work or may seem to be working when in fact the opposite effect is taking place. It goes something like the following:
>
> *Threads that pull blocks.* Sometimes what we draw from our experience might seem to us to be ways of connecting with the people we are interacting with; but we might miscalculate, and they actually create blocks.

Threads that pull blocks

An example of threads that pull blocks might be where the thread is drawn to share experiences but pulls with it an essentialist, Centre, large culture frame. This can be seen in the following reconstructed ethnographic account.[4] The main character is Kati, who was introduced in the two

---

3 http://adrianholliday.com/blocking-threads-and-threading-blocks/
4 This is based on observation of, and conversations with, postgraduate students constructing and reconstructing their intercultural identities while studying abroad, and also the experience of attending conference papers.

ethnographic accounts in Chapter 1. As Matt consults her in the second account in Chapter 1, she consults her friend Eli:

> As part of her masters course in intercultural communication, Kati has read about 'blocks' and 'threads'. Indeed, her supervisor has asked her to carry out a small piece of research in which she should practice 'drawing threads' with someone from a different cultural background. She has been warned not to talk explicitly about 'other cultures'; and she thinks that she is beginning to get her head around why – not to be essentialist by imagining that people are completely confined and definable by stereotypes. A good person for her to do this with is another student, Eli. They meet frequently anyway to share their experiences of what it is like to be away from home in a strange country. Even though they come from, as they often say, 'opposite ends of the world', they seem to have much in common. Finding threads should not therefore be difficult for them.
>
> They meet in the café and decide that what they are looking for should be simple, that is, not too political. They both come from big cities and discover that a thread that they can share is problems with rubbish, or garbage collection, as Kati prefers to call it. After a while they find themselves being quite negative as they start saying things like, 'Yes, in my culture nobody really cares about public places and about keeping them clean and tidy – not like Western countries where everything seems to work.' It's at this point that Eli says that they should slow down. She notices that this is the first time that they've been thinking about themselves as 'worse' or 'inferior' to people in the West, even though that's how they know that they are often constructed by people here.
>
> Kati agrees with her and then wonders if this 'thread' thing is a good idea if it just leads them to see the 'blocks' of how they are different to other people who wouldn't identify with their threads. But Eli disagrees with her. She says that they should try and do it differently. She reminds Kati that they've both heard people here also complain about rubbish. Even though here it looks much tidier and cleaner than at home, perhaps the real thread is trying to work out what they have in common. Then she remembers her mother saying that when foreigners visit their country she hopes that they will appreciate that the problems that they have – like rubbish, power cuts, overcrowded trains – are not because of their culture but because of their government.
>
> Then Kati realises what she should write in her assignment. She has to work out what it means when Eli's mother talks about 'their culture',

which also might be a bit essentialist. However, she can write about how problems with rubbish collection everywhere are connected with issues like governmental policy and efficiency. Even in this 'Western' country (because she's also supposed to interrogate what *that* means), you see rubbish lying around everywhere, even though everything is supposed to work so well and people look down on people like her and Eli for being 'uncivilised'.

The account demonstrates how finding threads can be, and perhaps *should* be, a struggle. It might also be significant that although Kati and Eli try to keep away from politics, which themselves raise Centre themes that connect with national and 'West versus the rest' discourses, they are certainly there as they try to break out of a more parochial 'us'-'them' discourse – thus demonstrating that talking about culture can never be neutral. Eli's mother's use of the word 'culture' needs to be thought about in this respect.

Adrian picks up the theme of struggle as he continues with his blog:

> This is why it can be such a struggle. We really need to think hard, to work out what really might connect. And even then, our theories and hypotheses about the other person might still be all wrong. This might be something to do with imposing images of the world that might not be as shared as we imagine. This is why we really do need to look deeper to find what actually we can share.
>
> Sometimes of course it just might not be possible. There might be incompatibilities that just cannot be overcome, and we have to walk away. And it might be insurmountable boundaries that are constructed by the other person. Of course, none of this might have anything to do with cultural background. But there are things going on in the world that are setting up huge walls of cultural – perhaps claiming to be religious – division.

The point that threads might not always be possible because of what amount to Centre forces is an important one. This is something that educators and researchers who wish to help students to find threads or set up circumstances for researching them need to consider. Just finding commonalities is not what this is about and can easily descend into 'comparing cultures'. Centre and deCentred forces have to be understood and considered. However, Kati and Eli, because they persist and do not give up, do manage to find a thread, though not quite the same as the one that they started out with.

Blocking threads

The blog continues to set out how blocks and threads may be manipulated for political and ideological purposes.

> *Blocking threads.* There might also be threads that are set up primarily for the purpose of constructing division and aggression. People are reached out to by others for the purpose of being pulled into massive blocks – establishments of state, nationalism, religion, values. There are clear examples of these in our history; and there are others upon us now. Indeed, what we know about the dangers of essentialism and Othering, about extreme Self and Other politics, provide those who have the ingenuity to dominate with the technologies to do so.

This is illustrated in the continuation of the account of Kati and her assignments:

> Kati had another assignment for her masters programme, this time to analyse a text from the media which had cultural and political connotations. She chose a BBC News article that critiqued an anti-migration poster supporting the British 'Brexit' campaign to leave the European Union.[5]
>
> It was actually the poster that most interested her more than what the article said about it. She came from a country that she felt had particularly suffered from migration to the extent that it had recently tried to close its borders. She was still thinking about the 'threads' idea. It helped her to explain how there were people here who shared her anxieties about migration. This poster was clearly meant to attract support from the people there because of their particular history rather than from her; but its slogan, 'We must break free … and take back control', spoke to her too. What she shared with a lot of people she met here was a feeling that their 'culture' was being lost because there were so many foreigners.
>
> However, when she told Eli what she was thinking, Eli was horrified. She said that Kati was falling into the same trap as before in their discussion about garbage collection. How could Kati ignore the racist implications of the poster, which the BBC News article explained very well? Eli said that if this was anything to do with threads, they were false threads that were seducing her into a racist discourse, and that this was the power of the poster. Eli said that in her country they were

5 https://www.theguardian.com/politics/2016/jun/16/nigel-farage-defends-ukip-breaking-point-poster-queue-of-migrants?CMP=Share_iOSApp_Other

only just recovering from an awful period of history in which half the population had been pulled together by an ideological 'thread'. It had initially seemed attractive because it helped them put aside cultural differences, but it had demonised the other half of the population and resulted in civil war.

There is very clearly a cultural thread in the anti-migration poster because it connects with lots of people, as indeed it is designed to do. However, because it is a Centre narrative that is perceived by lots of people to be a deCentred narrative because of its resistance to other Centre narratives, it is a *blocking* thread that is clearly massively destructive in that it represents an essentialist grand narrative of nation and culture. It is however on the surface in the sense that many people are aware of its ideological positionality. Kati is fortunate to have Eli to point these things out to her; and the discussion between them will continue. As the BBC News article itself states, the emergence of the poster actually caused politicians who also supported Brexit to distance themselves from its racist implications. That of course is by no means the end of the story. People who distance themselves from the more extreme anti-migration narrative may be in denial of a deeper, less visible neo-racism that hides beneath a neoliberal, West as steward discourse of patronage, as discussed earlier.

Threading blocks

Perhaps even more worrying is the case of something far more embedded and reified, as the blog goes on to explain:

> *Threading blocks.* In a very depressing scenario, this is where situations of violence and the cultural and political blocks of extreme identity and values construction, such as referred to above, have sustained for so long that young people have grown up with them and know little else. And what else they have experienced is coloured by extreme education. In such situations, the only threads that especially young people might have experience of are blocks.

Here, the Centre becomes invisible. An example of this becomes clear in Kati's response to Eli's criticism of her missing the point of the poster and not seeing its racism. There is also a strong element of third space in Kati's struggle to find a way:

> Kati was used to Eli rebuffing what she said in this way. They both came from societies that had been fraught with political and social

conflict to the extent that young people of their generation were highly politicised in their discussions. Kati and Eli often shared the irony that in their new country of study they were often labelled as being 'uncritical'. They had this reputation because they felt that some of the discussions in class were somehow too contrived; and they couldn't be bothered to participate. However, Kati was deeply concerned about a particular issue with Eli which Eli herself just didn't seem able to see.

Now that she was beginning, ironically with the help of Eli, to appreciate the full implication of the thread concept, it was providing her with a language with which to express what seemed problematic about Eli. This was what seemed to be Eli's very deep-seated prejudice against particular religious groups and gender roles and orientations within her own country. Eli didn't often mention this; but it did come out between the lines and in occasional throw-away statements that she made – comparing people that she didn't like with a particular class or people from a particular region, and certainly sometimes sounding quite homophobic. Kati could put this prejudice under the heading of a thread because she had met people from a range of cultural backgrounds who seemed to hold these views. Kati also felt it was very different to her prejudice about migration and nation in that Eli's prejudice seemed very ancient. Eli seemed to attribute these beliefs to religious teaching; but Kati was not convinced by this explanation because she was herself, she felt, religious, but had begun to work out the difference between specific teaching and much older cultural practice. Perhaps now that she had suffered Eli's attack against her own racism, Kati could now take courage to begin to challenge Eli, but more in her own mind than coming out and telling Eli what she thought.

Despite the friends' very clear shared deCentred resistance against the Centre, West as steward discourse of criticality, there is also a huge subjectivity regarding the other things that are going on between them. It is one interpretation of what two young people from diverse cultural backgrounds are observed to think and say about each other and about other people and ideas. The real events on which the account is based are themselves open to multiple interpretations. Regarding the last part especially, it is certainly possible that Kati has misunderstood Eli's positionality and is making essentialist, Othering assumptions about how Eli relates to a particular set of people and their ideological position. We would need to see what happens next as they develop their discussion. We know nothing of what is going on in their minds; we can only hear what they say.

This uncertainty in what might be going on relates to the overall aim of this book, which is to explore and to find a methodology and mechanisms with which to explore. Nevertheless, the analysis of this reconstructed ethnographic account does itself take a particular position – that essentialism and any associated Centre prejudice such as racism are not only inappropriate, but methodologically unsound.

Talking to Wissaal about clothes: threads of ambivalence

The discussion of blocks and threads and their associated narratives and positionings now continue as informed by our real-life interview with Wissaal, who is a recently arrived study-abroad postgraduate researcher.[6] We are interested in what she has to say about her experience of intercultural travel. In the first extract, Adrian raises the question of cultural artefacts as a way into the discussion – about how far we are prepared to wear clothing that seems to belong to a particular place. The topic quickly generates a common thread of ambivalent cultural experience that resonates richly with the cultural experience of all three participants as they genuinely look to each other for meanings:

Adrian: ok. If you- if you're on the aeroplane- and I went to Morocco recently. So the people travelling back on the aeroplane were carrying things that they'd bought. So they'd bought a camel or a donkey or something for their head. And this was something Moroccan- but they were just wearing it like a- like an object. They weren't being Moroccan because they were wearing these things. And I don't think it would be easy for them to be- to do anything that was Moroccan without looking like that. And I think this is a very important question. If Sara did something which was from your country you'd probably laugh. You'd say that this isn't real. This is silly.

Sara: well this depends on the context. I mean if I do it now for example you might laugh. But if I'm in your country maybe this might be interpreted as something that I'm doing to to interact better. So it can be appreciated for example. Can it be? I'm just imagining- so-

Wissaal: yes. This is what we come back to another question. Are you ready to wear something different?

Adrian: to wear something different?

Wissaal: to wear something different. It's very individualistic I think.

Sara: yea I think for example- for example for me it would- I would be- it would be easier for me for example to- for example to listen to other

---

6 The material presented here comes from the larger research project reported in two recent publications (Amadasi & Holliday 2017, 2018). Wissaal is a pseudonym.

kinds of music for example. I don't know yet about where it may be. I mean I tried, for example when I was in- when I was in Senegal I tried to wear Senegalese dresses. But of course I felt like- I felt pretty ridiculous because I knew that other people were looking at me as- as yes

Adrian: ((laughing))

Sara: actually I'm ((laughing)) contradicting what I just said. So yea ((laughing)) I mean I was there and I tried to wear like a Senegalese woman but of course I felt ridiculous

Wissaal: yes. But you felt that you want to try it

Throughout this extract there is an intense interplay of grand and personal narratives which creates a good example of threading blocks as discussed earlier. The essentialist, Centre grand narrative which reduces 'other cultures' to their national costumes, a process which has been critiqued by a number of people (Kumaravadivelu 2007: 109), is what Adrian is intending to critique in his description of tourists wearing Moroccan artefacts to test Wissaal's response. Sara follows by querying how she would be regarded doing this when visiting Wissaal's country, and then refers to her own experience of doing this while visiting Senegal, possibly falling into the trap of threading blocks.

Wissaal's 'Are you ready to wear something different?' expresses a thread to Adrian's experience, but, with 'It's very individualistic, I think', introduces a personal narrative of individuality that distances her from the grand narrative. It might be the case that Wissaal reproduces individualism to be a Centre narrative. It is not clear whether this is in response to our critique and querying; but throughout this section the two types of narratives form an intense twine in which all parties show their uncertainties. Sara laughs at how she herself talks so easily about how to recognise a 'Senegalese women' in terms of what she wears and the essentialist meaning that this claim might imply. The laughing and Wissaal's empathising 'but you felt' show all three participants sharing their struggle, as a third space emerges. Their struggle is with the not inconsiderable problem of how to appreciate difference, which *is* often expressed through clothing, and of how foreigners cannot just imitate without looking 'ridiculous', as Adrian intimates at the beginning of the event.

'Wearing shorts' and threads of non-participation

What has so far been a largely researcher-led interview event begins to take on a greater life of its own in which Wissaal takes us researchers with her in an ambivalent negotiation of grand and personal narratives about clothing

choices and annoyances. A few lines before the following extract: Adrian
has commented on the differences between how men and women dress. He
says that, while many of the women in the students' group of which Wissaal
is a member dress in a way that is visibly particular to their group, the men
do not. This intervention thus openly introduces the issue of gender, which
had remained implicit until that point. While Adrian intends this to be a
thread, there are clear dangers in alluding to gender differences that might
be construed as blocks. Perhaps each person in the conversation sees the
other as representing a Centre narrative about gender representation and is
therefore trying to deCentre it as the third space struggle continues.

This may or may not be the reason why Wissaal now talks about wom-
en's clothes and her issues with shorts, and then brings this back to gender
difference:

Wissaal: yes the most noticeable clothes we can see on women from this
country elsewhere even here is the short

Sara: mm

Wissaal: in cultural words- this is very cultural word because in Turkey I've
seen many people from here- ladies all people are a bit conservative
when it comes to clothing but ladies- British and Germanic people
wear short ((unclear))

Sara: mm

Wissaal: so always noticeable and when I came here- when I come here
maybe in the summer where there is- when we have the sunny day I
notice the same thing

Sara: mm

Wissaal: yes. The short is commonly dressed by most of the ladies but with
the gentlemen in my group wear the t-shirts and trousers is what we
have in- this is our way

Adrian: but if you see them on the street here

Wissaal: yes

Adrian: they seem like everyone else

Wissaal: yes

Adrian: in their clothing

Wissaal: yees ((questioning))

Adrian: but but you don't look like everyone- everybody else in your
clothing

Wissaal: yees

Adrian: so there's something different between the women

Wissaal: and men

Adrian: and the men

In the first four turns Wissaal introduces wearing shorts as something which pertains to women and in particular Western women. However, in her fourth turn she mentions Adrian's argumentation, which overtakes the difference between Western and non-Western, to focus rather on the difference between male and female concerning what they wear. He is pushing the third space to get to the bottom of what is going on with regard to the shorts.

Sara takes advantage of the issue of gender that has just emerged to develop it as a thread with Wissaal, who claims that the difference between Western and non-Western women is subsumed beneath a 'female reflexivity' on how to dress. With her first and longest turn, Sara therefore tries to suggest a thread between her and Wissaal which cuts across the dichotomy between Western and non-Western. Although Sara might be considered as a Western woman, she emphasises that she does not like to wear shorts either:

Sara: yes I was wondering- when you told about the shorts that actually for me for example- when you asked me whether I can switch- I can change my way of of dressing- Sorry there is a telephone ringing (.) And I realise that it's- it would be easier- it would be harder for me to dress in shorts for example 'cause I can't- I mean I don't like them so I would feel not comfortable with myself although here in- also in Italy they are very common so yes I don't know but it would be easier for me to dress a traditional dress of any other kind of places rather than for example shorts. I don't know why so I just- yes.

Adrian: I also find it very difficult to wear shorts

Wissaal: yes I have shorts at home

Adrian: ((laughing))

Wissaal: too

Adrian: ((laughing))

Wissaal: I have different colours

Sara: erm

Wissaal: when I was younger I didn't put the veil. The veil I put it just lately

Adrian: ah

Wissaal: I used to swim by shorts. I used to go to the- to the beach by shorts

Sara: ah

Wissaal: but now I've changed

Adrian: ((laughing))

Wissaal: because of my decision to put the veil

Adrian: yes

Wissaal: so

Sara: yes yes- I mean I was wearing them when I was younger but now I don't feel comfortable any more so yes I don't wear them any- anymore.

I don't feel like- I like myself with this kind of dress. So yes I don't know where we are going

Adrian: ((laughing)) yes

Wissaal: it depends. It depends. If you don't like your body to appear or nearly the ((laughing))

Adrian: ((laughing))

Sara: ((laughing))

Wissaal: the parts of your body to be showed maybe here you would say I will not dress the short

Adrian: yes

Sara: yes, yes

Wissaal: it's individualistic

Sara: yes

Wissaal: there is nothing to do with the- with culture

Adrian: ok. So you're- you're saying something different now

Sara: mmm

As Sara and Wissaal engage in this thread, Adrian breaks in with nervous laughs which seem to indicate he is now an outsider, perhaps blocked by their threading talk in which he thinks that they are taking a new Centre ground. At one point, his attempted thread state`t that he also does not like to wear shorts does not seem to be picked up and seems to enforce his outsider position. Therefore, the thread between Sara and Wissaal seems to be built on belonging to the same gender. The way this becomes visible is that, suddenly, the issue about whether to wear shorts or not is discussed only by the two women of the group, Sara and Wissaal, restricting Adrian's participation in the discussion, which goes on as a 'woman issue' for a few lines.

We could therefore say that even blocks and threads cannot be defined in an *a priori* way; but they force us to look at participants' reactions and positioning to evaluate their effects. In this case, for example, although Sara's intervention builds a thread which allows her and Wissaal to leave religion and national culture outside their narrated style choices, it is a thread that pulls an essentialist gender block that implies that only women have the body issues connected with wearing shorts. This eventual block narrative, which Adrian tries to interrupt through his intervention 'I also find it very difficult to wear shorts', as every block narrative, risks leaving people outside the conversation, because it looks at them as merely members of a specific social group, without considering individual personal trajectories or experiences that cross expected structural lines. In this third space, the politics of the Centre and the deCentred continues. Indeed, this might be an inevitable, natural politics of positioning that will take place everywhere if allowed.

Moreover, it is relevant to consider the ambivalence of Wissaal's reaction to Sara's narrative in which they are setting up their own third space that excludes Adrian. Firstly, she confirms Sara's narrative which tries to break the dichotomy between Western and non-Western woman, by saying that she used to wear shorts as well. This alignment is however contradicted a few turns later when she introduces the issue of the veil as a moment of change in her dressing choices. This reference to religious belief represents a mitigated distance from Sara's narrative by introducing a new personal one, which is guided by religion, and therefore could be argued to be a splinter of the grand essentialist narrative. This claim is not however definitive, as in the last turns, Wissaal affirms the individuality of this choice by distancing herself from any cultural influence and confirming the thread to Sara's narrative. Third-space ambivalence therefore continues.

This movement amongst different and also potentially competing narratives is an important element to be analysed to comprehend social events as small culture formation on the go. It may be the case that Wissaal is bringing an element of belief to the conversation in her reference to a moment in her life in which she decides to wear the veil; but she nevertheless brings a wider discursive element to the issue that connects with personal elements that Sara and Adrian bring to the conversation. It may also be the case that Sara and Adrian exaggerate their own statements slightly in order to engage with the conversation and to carry it on to the everyday ambivalences that we all might have regarding wearing shorts. However, this is something that we all might do in any conversation as we respond to each other and have the desire to 'make' conversation. Wissaal may also be doing this. We do not wish to dwell on what this person or that believes about wearing shorts. Rather, we wish to draw attention to how three people, each with their own cultural history, come together to make the conversation. That Wissaal, at least for a moment, states that this has nothing to do with 'culture' and that it is all 'individualistic', might indicate that she is diving into the mêlée of sense-making. This might however just be a momentary departure from an essentialist block.

What is important here is that the interview provides a small culture environment in which three people work hard to negotiate meanings through agency. We three participants are working to engage with each other by investigating each other's narratives. We each operate a form of 'prudence' through which we are all investigating each other's expectations. To do this, we draw from particular elements of our lives outside the interview. This is indeed the nature of the third space.

The shared uncertainties that Wissaal, Sara and Adrian find themselves engaged with become, to use Leonard Cohen's (1992) expression, the cracks that let in the light of a wider world. Light implies a positive. And here, we authors, Sara and Adrian, must come out and declare the positive spin that we place on an exploratory conversation that implies agency rather than a probable 'descent' into essentialist blocks. It is therefore in a sense our victory that the interview is a place in which Wissaal finds it important to express what she seems to imply, through her own emphasis, to be extreme individuality.

All parties in the interview are caught in nuances of difference. All our reasons for doing things are conflicted to the extent that we bring out different layers at different times – for example belief and aesthetics – and all appropriate as long as not interfering with the liberties of others.

Behind the scenes: sense-making of threads or not threads

As with Sara's research with the Italian schoolchildren in Chapter 2, to pursue the nature of the research interview as small culture formation on the go, it is important to take it beyond the transcribed interview data. It is not possible for us researchers to know what was behind Wissaal's responses; but we can explore what our own generate. It is important for us to stand back to make private sense of what is going on; and we look at our email correspondence in which we make sense of where there are threads and where there are not, to work out the deeper rules.

The following is an email exchange between Sara and Adrian trying to make sense of the interview with Wissaal as they talk about their analysis of it. We have presented it as a dialogue which reveals something of how we as researchers work with the uncertainty of how to make sense:

Adrian: I think that this is now almost there. I like the way you have managed the very complex weave. I've edited it just a bit for expression and put in a couple of blue changes and comments – in one place making the male exclusion case a bit stronger.

Sara: I don't know. I was thinking about it concerning the last extract, where Wissaal doesn't seem to 'accept' my thread, by introducing the element of belief. Anyway, I worked again on it. Let me know what you think about it. I see it now taking finally a shape and this makes me feel relieved.

Adrian: you mean if the thread is sent out but isn't picked up? I guess we never know how far threads are picked up. I don't see why a large part of the thread can't be the intention to make connection. We can only try. So, yes, I would think it's still a thread. I'm pleased you wanted to comment so positively. I was worried for a moment that you didn't like it.

Sara: I have just thought something. If Sara tries to build a thread through a narrative, but Wissaal doesn't align to this narrative, is it still a thread?I mean, did we write somewhere about the interactive need of the thread to be a thread? And is it something relevant in your opinion?

PS: I would have only written that, in this process of getting to understand each other's thoughts, what was meaningful was also that, in order to be clearer to the other, we maybe have to understand better ourselves too. But it was too obvious and naïve this is why I didn't write it at the end.

Adrian: oh dear. What comment would you make?

Sara: yes I read both of them. I was tempted to comment, but then I enjoyed the role of the 'remained in obscurity' co-writer. I changed a bit this morning, but now I feel I need to go back to the audio file for this veil issue. There is something still not clear to me about it. I will go back after the listening, hopefully with some (good) ideas!

There are a number of things to note here that throw further light on the nature of qualitative interpretation and indeed of the uncertain nature of threads and the nuances of the third space.

The benefit of having two co-writers is noticeable. It is clear that Sara and Adrian are prepared to 'tweak', add comment to and validate each other's interpretation. Adrian mentioning that he has tweaked the analysis in the text to draw attention to the gender issue around the wearing of shorts, which we will return to again later, should not be seen as manipulating the text for his own purposes. His sharing of this with Sara, and her sharing with him what she is thinking and doing about what they write, is a genuine dialogue of sense-making. This is not just to do with the role and power of writing in research, but with how we all make sense of the social world in small culture formation on the go in, to greater or lesser degrees, conversation with each other.

Resonating with the analysis of Sara and Adrian interviewing each other in Chapter 4 is Sara noting that 'in order to be clearer to the other, we maybe have to understand better ourselves too'. Here she is concerned with whether threads have to be received as such before they can really be considered to be threads. It is not just a matter of whether or how they are picked up, but also the nature of their intent. There is also the luxury of being able to go back to the interview transcript 'hopefully' to get 'some [good] ideas'. In most of our everyday encounters, we are not able to do this. However, how much time do we spend replaying what we have seen, heard and said in our heads to evaluate what we should do next?

In another email exchange, we go deeper into our own feelings about the interview. This regards specifically Adrian looking as though he was not included in the discussion about not wanting to wear shorts. He and Sara have of course already spoken about this. Sara emails:

Sara: I think I understood why you were laughing nervously: because we were cutting you out from the conversation! If you look at the turns, you don't speak anymore, and all the issue is between me and Wissaal because of that gender issue we talked about yesterday.

I tried to give a sense to this, also by re-listening to our interview. This is why I describe also what happened before, where you speak about the differences in women's and men's clothing. I don't know, I think it might help to go on, but I also think that I can improve it a bit. But first I'd need to know if you agree on what I have written so far.

Sara is again revisiting what she has written about this in her interpretation. Interestingly, in his response, Adrian, at this point does not seem so worried about it, but does refer to a personal thread back to his own experience:

Adrian: that's interesting. I don't remember being felt left out: but being someone who doesn't like to be associated with an image of men inhabiting a different world to women, I would naturally want to draw a thread from my own very personal reasons for not wanting to wear shorts.

It needs to be remembered here that 'getting to the bottom of things' can also only be taken so far. As time passes, our memories about what we thought and meant at a particular time and the reasons why will change. Within the social science researcher agenda, as perhaps different to other agendas, the aim is not to understand what people did in the sense of 'who did it', as might be the case for example with criminal investigation. The purpose of this discussion is instead to lay bare the nature of how we all interact with each other in small culture formation on the go and not the specifics of individual agendas *per se*. It might be that the research setting, as well as showing small culture formation on the go, should, by its very nature, be a third space in the sense that it would always be ambivalent and awkward. It should also be deCentred, as that is what making the familiar (Centre) strange is all about.

Kati, Eli and Matt visit 'the foreign': blocks and threads at work

As a concluding section for this chapter, the following reconstructed ethnographic account explores how blocks and threads can operate when Kati and her fellow students go on a class field trip to a location that is culturally strange in different ways for all of them:[7]

> Kati was given another assignment for her intercultural communication course, to go with a group of friends from different cultural backgrounds to a place which was 'foreign' to all of them and to write an ethnographic account of their experience. She was of course told to problematise what 'foreign' might mean; and she felt that this would be easy for her after all the confusing encounters and discussions that the course had already led her into. She was also told to read Gerd Baumann's ethnography of the London suburb of Southall, *Contesting Culture*, from which she had gleaned something about the complex ways in which people could think and talk about culture, and how the researcher should put aside their own prior thoughts about things that might colour how they saw them. With all of this in mind, she asked her friend Eli to go with her, plus a 'local' student called Matt with whom she had recently made friends to the extent that they sometimes texted to share what he referred to as 'intercultural experiences'. Again, she wasn't any longer sure what 'local' meant; but she felt that he was 'Western', unlike her and Eli; and she was curious about how he would respond, and also from a male perspective.
>
> Their university was in a large industrial city that had a number of neighbourhoods with what seemed to her to be distinct 'migrant' communities. This was where Matt was particularly useful. He was a cultural studies student and was even more critical than her tutor about the way that people were labelled. She was pleased that he hadn't come out with the normal veiled racist interrogation about where she came from and a suggestion that she might need help with the library. He said he knew a place where they should go, which was populated largely by people with South Asian heritage, and where even he, who came from this part of the country, felt quite foreign.
>
> The three of them went by bus and walked around the three main shopping streets. They stopped to look in shop windows and walked through several indoor markets. Kati took photos with her phone and said that they were supposed to record their conversations about what they thought. They stopped at a small café in an indoor market and ordered pastries and coffee.

---

7 This narrative is based on the experience of ourselves and postgraduate students' short-term travel to foreign locations.

Kati could sense that Matt was uncomfortable. When she asked him how he felt, he said that he felt totally out of place and that people could recognise that he was an outsider and only there to look at them as though they were in a fishbowl. She was interested that he didn't include her and Eli as 'the foreigners' in this observation. Perhaps he thought that they looked like the people there. He had asked for decaffeinated coffee and they didn't have it. He said that the man behind the counter didn't seem to know what it was and that this showed that the people here didn't consider themselves part of Western society. He then went on about what he referred to as 'these 1950s mannequins of blond women'. Kati has also noticed them because there were quite a lot of them. Around where they were sitting there was a line of shops that sold material for women's clothes. Kati said that they had them in similar shops where she came from so she hadn't really noticed. Matt said that they looked as though they were made in the 1950s, but that what was really noticeable was that many of them had blond hair and blue eyes and that this made him think that there was a duplicity in 'the culture' where many of the women customers seemed quite religious and were covered – something to do with 'using quaint Western images to sell traditional clothes'. Later on, when she was writing her assignment, Kati found a picture on the internet of mannequins like the ones they were talking about.

At this point, Eli, who had so far not said much at all, broke into the conversation and said that she felt Matt was just looking for the exotic and was constructing 'images of "backwardness"'. She said that not having sophisticated coffee shops could be an act of resistance against globalisation. She said she wondered why he hadn't also mentioned the naked mannequins that she had noticed him glancing at in the shop window they passed before coming to the café, the image of which would have completed his Orientalist imaginings. She said that his image of 'duplicity' suggested that he had fallen right into the trap of thinking that everyone outside the West was 'collectivist' and therefore had to all behave in the same way. Just because some women wished to cover themselves didn't mean that they couldn't be part of a world with a multiplicity of images. She said that it was a Western preoccupation with Protestant singularity which allowed no room for saying one thing and doing another.

They quickly left the café; and, as they were walking along the street, they saw a woman standing at the edge of the pavement. They all thought she looked as though she belonged to the local community. She was shouting, 'I love my country. I can do whatever I like.' A man who was passing by on the other side of the pavement with two children slowed down and said to her, 'You need to be quiet. This is not appropriate. You cannot do just what you like.' The woman continued, repeating what she was shouting. Matt thought to himself that she was bravely stating her freedom in the face of hypocritical gender rules of the local community, which the man represented. Eli imagined that this would be what Matt would be thinking.

Kati imagined the same as Matt, but couldn't work out what Eli would think – whether she would agree with the man or with the woman. This left her with a feeling of ambivalence. Part of her also felt like a foreigner, but not because of what might usually be perceived as a cultural difference, as she thought Matt was referring to. She felt she was more captured by analysing differences between where she came from and here with regard to their stories as arrival countries for migrants, and how they structurally managed the issue of cultural difference. In some ways she felt less foreign in this suburb of a foreign country than she did in migrant suburbs of her own city due to the socio-economic isolation of some groups who lived there, from the rest of the city. Here she didn't feel that distance. She didn't feel the same economic-power diversity that she did at home.

She also agreed with Eli that Matt was looking for exoticness and imagining 'backward' duplicity rather than recognising the multiplicity of cultural forces. It had something to do with the woman shouting that she was free. She knew several of her fellow students who came from outside the West who talked about the freedom that they had here. She also, however, heard this from students who came from here – just because they were living away from their families for the first time. What they all had in common was simple things to do with getting on with life, like going to restaurants or concerts or parties when they wanted. It didn't have to be political. It was also something to do with the ordinariness of the actual realities of places – just people getting on with their lives and being who they are – perhaps projecting the icons of their pasts, but just like all of us do.

Thinking further about Matt, she felt that what Eli had asserted about his essentialism, about his Orientalism, was something that she and all her country-people had to learn to critique in themselves with regard to migrant populations in their midst. She wondered if she would have the courage to confront Eli herself about what she might not understand about her own deep prejudices. At the same time, she might learn that Eli wasn't as essentialist as she thought.

The reference to Gerd Baumann's (1996) ethnography, also referred to in Chapter 1, describes how local residents engage in everyday contestation of the established essentialist view of culture within shifting multicultural communities. This reconstructed ethnographic account is, however, less about what the suburb that the three students visited was like, but rather about the nature of the blocks and threads which are in operation in the small culture formation on the go where the three of them relate to each other. It is useful here to summarise their different perspectives:

- Eli is initially critical of an easy approach to threads that simply compares similar things across national culture blocks. She also sees the dangers of ideological attempts to use racist threads to manipulate people. She is critical of Matt's exoticisation of the migrant community they 'visit'. She, however, also has deep-seated prejudices against particular groups, including migrants, in her own society.
- Kati learns from Eli and moves from seeing threads as blocking comparisons and sharing of prejudices to a struggle to find underlying commonalities that cross large culture boundaries.
- Matt is sensitive to the Othering politics of labelling. He seems, however, to be quite disparaging about the migrant 'culture' that they 'visit'.

Table 3.1 tries to rationalise the complex shades of blocks and threads that have emerged throughout the chapter with reference to Kati's interactions with her friends and the choices in perception that they represent.

It is important to reflect more on the example of Matt. He is the only person we actually *hear* speaking to the others about his experience in the suburb. First, he represents a warning about political correctness. There is a hint at the beginning of the account that he is the one who is wary, and the one Kati relies on for the politics of labels and how safely to refer to the people living in the suburb. There is a danger here of constructing a neoliberal technology of labels that then makes us think that we have solved the problem. It seems that he has learnt how to address Kati in a way that does not make her feel Othered, but this awareness does not prevent him from falling into an essentialist trap later on. This might mean that threads cannot be achieved by following other people's rules. They have to be on a personal level.

Regarding Eli, her self-stated non-Western status would seem to make it easier for her to arrive consciously at some sort of deCentred position. However, like Matt, she may not have had someone to challenge her. As Kati notes, she does not seem to realise her own deep prejudices about ethnic and gender minorities in her own society that might be far worse than Matt's prejudices about 'foreigners'. None of us should be complacent about what we might or might not be prejudiced about.

However, similarly, we as researchers would like to point out the relevance of evaluating the ability of the characters in the account to deal

Table 3.1 Complex shades

Threads	Effect
Unspoken, observed	
Kati inviting the other students to go on the field trip	Revealing conflicts between Matt and Eli, and Matt's essentialism
Kati asking the other students about their experience of the suburb	Kati understanding different types of foreignness
Kati resonating with Eli's critique of Matt's essentialism	Kati understanding the normal everyday cultural complexity of people everywhere
Kati connecting her experience of the suburb with her experience of suburbs with migrant communities at home	Kati connecting with the structure of prejudice at home
Kati connecting the experience of freedom between the woman in the street, other students studying abroad, students 'here' away from home for the first time	Kati appreciating the interculturality of freedom
Possible choices of action	
Kati sharing her insights about the structures of migration at home with Eli	Perhaps enabling Eli to see her own prejudices
	Perhaps getting beyond Eli's apparent essentialism
Kati talking to both foreign and home students about their experiences of freedom	Appreciating freedom as a transcendent intercultural quality

with threads and blocks not as an innate individual ability but as a sensitive reflexive attitude that has to be trained and interactionally applied. This is the reason why the characters in the account sometimes present ambivalent behaviour: this feature is important to breaking down essentialising constructions of individual prototypes and highlighting how contradicting and overlapping positionings can be taken up by the same person at once within a third space.

What becomes evident in searching for the threads in the account is that they do not always have to be acted out in speech. Apart from Matt's statement and Eli's rebuff, the content of the account is what Kati is thinking about the others and the place. As the second part of Table 3.1 suggests, this thinking, this reflection, this reflexivity, provides Kati with plans for where she might take action with threads in the future. Therefore, while threads can be created in our mind, it is only when they become interactionally shared in the occasion of small culture formation that we can see their effect on the building of interculturality.

Building interculturality

In this chapter, we have shown that there is a strong relationship between small culture formation on the go and interculturality. This is not only due to the fact that small culture formation on the go is the essence of inter-cultural engagement. While it can be argued that all cultural encounters are in effect intercultural and that the basic enablers of this intercultural engagement are threads and the avoidance of blocks, it is specifically in the act of threading and block avoidance that the basis for interculturality lies. Interculturality can be conceived thus not as a pre-existing condition that needs to be achieved, but rather as the result of a series of specific interactional choices, and, therefore, as an expression of agency. Indeed, the building of threads is the basis for the building of interculturality. It implies reflexivity and creativity. However, these two concepts need to be used not as a mere style exercise. They need to be coordinated through interaction, in which ongoing attention to the other participants' and the relevance of attending to what others say are valued as elements which make a difference in the interactional event itself – in the process of meaning construction and finally on the road to building interculturality.

4   Who are we as researchers?

In the last chapter, we looked at how the people we engage with in research settings employ block and thread narratives in complex ways to position themselves both with each other and with researchers. In this chapter, we will look at how researchers also do this – just like the people they research. Unlike the dynamics studied in previous chapters, because all the participants are researchers, they start their interactions with a degree of commonality in the discourses and narratives that they share that are linked to their academic community. This means that by considering how participants splinter personal from grand narratives, through the interplay of personal cultural trajectories and influences from the media, education and other national and international sources, researchers' sharing of certain words, ideas and concepts as an academic group has a particular role in the construction and reproduction of the narratives. This will allow us to reflect on how an apparently homogenous group of researchers can engage in negotiations that contribute to the creation of uncomfortable deCentred third spaces. Their experience of this is relevant for their understanding of the people they research and will research in the future.

The events in this chapter are therefore: email interviews which Adrian carried out with postgraduate researchers studying abroad at a British university; a face-to-face interview that we carried out with one of the postgraduate researchers; and face-to-face interviews which we two researchers carried out with each other. Adrian asked the postgraduate researchers to talk about how personal cultural trajectories became major resources in carrying out their research into various aspects of what might, hesitantly, be termed 'travel to the West'. In addition, we asked the postgraduate researcher in the face-to-face interview what she had learnt from engaging with her participants about her hopes and anxieties, the cultural identity that brought to her research, how she managed the balance between the interpersonal and the researcher role, and what she generally found important in her research. The postgraduate researchers asked for their real names to be used and research projects to be mentioned.

Important to note here is the signalling of personal cultural trajectories not only in cultural travel, but also in researching cultural travel. This sets up a major theme of this chapter – the relationship between researching and what we all do in how we negotiate the intercultural. Secondly, 'travel to the West', while recognised as a problematic concept, signals a sense of cultural displacement or strangeness which is necessary to denote a relationship between Self and Other with a sufficient degree of uncertainty and indeed deCentredness to enable a reflexive third space. This displacement was very evident in the events in Chapter 1, not only in the case of Kati in Exia, and with the distant time and place of being a slave in pre-Columbian Texas, but also with Matt on the train in his country of birth, in Sara's positioning being initially rejected by her participants in Chapter 2, and in Kati and Eli's interrogation of their own identities in Chapter 3. There is also the necessary inclusivity, which runs throughout the book, where the postgraduate researchers are recognised as 'expert researchers', just as the children with migration backgrounds in Chapter 2 are recognised from the outset as expert cultural travellers.

Cultural travel is seen to be taking place within the process of the interviews, as we all move out from the predefined interview questions to explore with emergent and more pointed questions aspects which arise. Our analysis will therefore focus on the dialogic process between us – at how the told narratives weave with details of the specific moment, where the braiding, overlapping and unravelling of threads increases the range of resources and the possibilities of the narratives.

We therefore demonstrate how the research process itself with all the layers of reflection and social confrontations in the academic domain also depends on the particular process of small culture formation on the go. As suggested by McAdams and Logan (2006), academics' stories about their questions, doubts and ideas, and the ways they are integrated coherently in reflections concerning their life's choices and events, represent a good empirical opportunity to observe how people combine stories from different spheres of their life. By doing this, social researchers give voice to how they employ their own cultural travel in the investigation and observation of their participants' narratives. Their own stories become the light guiding them in the observation and analysis of the world around them. This personal-researcher relationship is the specific concern in auto/biography research (Merrill & West 2009) but it can also be the case for all constructivist ethnography, as discussed in Chapter 1. It is important to recognise researchers' belonging to and engagement with those same social processes they aim to study to avoid being seduced by the idea of positivist detachment. We struggle to find meanings and purposes in our lives while presenting a professional researcher identity to ourselves and our audience.

This belonging to the world that we research does not therefore invalidate our work. Rather, it is an admission of our ongoing interrogation of our own unavoidable relationship with Centre grand narratives and their attendant prejudices and stereotypes, and also with the identity requirements and those elements of our personal lives that are moulded and digested to become professional resources.

Excavating our own researcher agendas

First we will explore Sara's own positionality as a researcher in her interviews with Adrian. We see specific narratives that she brings to the interview and new ones that emerge as she negotiates her positionality during the interview. The interview extracts in this chapter will focus on narratives and the thematic journeys and shifts through which they move and develop instead of the interactional aspects that we looked at in Chapter 2. It is an important tenet of our argument that we do not conceive these narratives as individual stories created and situated in one specific person's head and then poured into the social event regardless of what is going on there. The narratives we investigate must therefore be considered inside a network of pre-existing social relationships and the shared knowledge which orientates them.

Moreover, when we interviewers move out from our predefined questions to explore with more pointed questions which arise during the interview, the analysis will focus not only on the interviewees' answers but also on the dialogical process between all the participants including ourselves. We will look at how the told narratives become a weave which is fed with details of the specific moment, where the braiding, overlapping and unravelling of threads coming from individuals communicating with each other increases the range of resources and possibilities for establishing third spaces.

Resisting positioning

Here, Sara and Adrian are talking about a piece of research that she carried out with undergraduate students. Even though they are both supposedly experts in the field who share a paradigmatic discourse, she resists the positioning that he tries to impose upon her – that she had some sort of special researcher eye that could reveal hidden realities:

Adrian: Because you were seeing things that they didn't see
Sara: No, actually, quite the opposite. I mean they saw things that I wasn't
    seeing

Sara resists his positioning through a 'dispreferred response' (Hester & Hester 2012) which openly presents an alternative issue to reflect upon. At the same time, what might be considered a 'pre-existing social condition' of two researchers with different academic status and English skills is not evident in the way that she resists his positioning of her. A Centre structuralist perspective would argue that such a differentiation in roles would have an *a priori* boundedness and effect. However, according to Henriksen (2008) the plot of the interaction allows unexpected positionings to emerge. We can therefore claim here that Sara's rejection of Adrian's positioning of her emerges from the situation itself and not from external structures, and that there is a possibility that the particular professional collaboration between them can be independent of the expected academic structure. Sara confirms that they have always collaborated as equal co-researchers. Moreover, as we can see in the following examples, their positionings are not fixed, but rather shifting rapidly from one turn to the other.

This can be seen a few minutes after the above exchange when positionings are put at stake and under negotiation again. The second agenda that Adrian tries to impose is that of the researcher involved in self-discovery, which Sara also rejects. The discussion becomes intense and initially it is Sara who tries to mitigate discordance as Adrian adopts a more conflictual attitude:

Adrian: If this researcher identity, which has something to do with not being quite socialised in the same way as other people and therefore you look at things in a questioning way a little bit more than other people might do- Does this mean that when you are researching other people, it's more to do with you understanding and sorting out yourself than it is understanding them? Are you- Therefore, is it fair to write about other people when really your agenda is understanding yourself?

Sara: Well, this is what is usually said about psychologists, I mean, many people I knew they were studying psychology, when you ask them why you study psychology they answered 'because I want to understand myself better' but I don't think it's my- I mean I don't want to understand myself better. It's not that I'm-

Sara's answer here tries softly to take distance from Adrian's suggested narrative. She does this by introducing another narrative which is however in danger of falling into the trap of stereotyping the category of 'psychologists', and thus might be considered a Centre block narrative. The mitigation here is thus realised both by turning the attention to something else (psychologists) instead of proposing a personal open position and with the use – once the personal position is introduced – of a very indirect form like 'I don't think it's my-'.

This hesitation in taking a position is interrupted by Adrian's intervention, where he opposes a clear contraposition by opening the turn with 'No OK':

Adrian: No OK. What I am getting at is- there is something immoral about looking at people around you and talking and writing about them and indirectly making judgements about them and their prejudices and their ideologies and all those things when really this is about you finding yourself? So, might they look at you and say 'how dare you say all these things about us when really it's you trying to work out how you should be?'

Sara: Well, but I don't think it's working out- working out how *I* should be I think it's working out how ehm society is and of course I'm inside it. So of course I'm involved in this process but it's not just- it's not just to understand me. It's maybe to understand me inside that processes-

Through a clear rejection in his turn, Adrian is potentially opening the field for a conflict. Sara's answer is still mitigating; although a clearer positioning is expressed and strongly chased by Adrian. He creates an oppositional narrative by constructing a fictionalised discussion among a group of people. They criticise social scientists' work and call into question their right to investigate forms of prejudices by distinguishing 'people who carry on research' and 'people upon whom the research is carried on'.

It is in response to this hypothetical block narrative that Sara is pushed to argue her positioning and to provide further details of her own narrative, which arrives in the following turns, with a more detailed theoretical explanation:

Adrian: But do you see what I mean by the morality? You see, I could

Sara: Yes yesyes-

Adrian: I could say to you 'look I know what I am doing I know how I am thinking, I have these prejudices I can manage all of this, you are the one who is making use of stories about my prejudices in order to sort yourself out. I am not the one with problems, you are the one with problems'

Sara: Yes but I still see a psychological perspective in this, because actually what I am looking at is not what's the problem or problems behind a single person, as well as it's not the problem behind me but rather- but rather how that view, problematic or not I don't know, how that affect the whole society and how it works in the society what creates in the relationship with others, so it's never just on the individual […]

The explanation given by Sara, concerning her way of approaching research and research participants, is of her theoretical choices and the attempt to create a coherent opposition to Adrian's hypothetical narrative. This is a moment in which doubts and beliefs that the two researchers have been having since they started their careers inside this field of study are expressed and socially unravelled. Each of their own personal narratives is processed through the mirror of the other.

The implication of this analysis is that it is possible, when the interlocutors choose to work hard to stand outside Centre structures, to arrive at a more creative, and hence deCentred, resolution and a dissolving of potential dissonances.

Negotiating researcher identities

What is also happening here is that the two researchers are engaged in interactively working out their professional identities. While we can never know how serious or how experimental this moment was, what we can focus on is how that local negotiated process of 'doing being' (Gafaranga 2001) is here deeply involved and observable.

A few minutes later, when the interview is approaching an end, Sara and Adrian reflect on what has just happened and they co-construct a meaning to the event they have been involved in:

Adrian: So one final question: how do you feel about this interview- because you look very disoriented and dishevelled
Sara: Well it was very good (but) at the very end I felt a little bit panicking yes
Adrian: Well you know if I am accusing you I am actually accusing myself
Sara: For a moment I could see that you were really trying to push me in a very difficult situation to see how I reacted

In the second turn, Adrian openly declares the contradiction in his own positionings. This turn is important because it opens a further possibility of discussion, as Sara's last turn shows. Here a personal interpretation of the conflictual moment of the event is given, providing an important glimpse for the analysis of the negotiation of the third space just seen.

Both Sara and Adrian need to think about Sara's reluctance to be positioned in relation to their strategy of intervention seen with the children with migration backgrounds in Chapter 2, between Kati and Eli in each of the reconstructed ethnographic accounts, and with study abroad students elsewhere (Amadasi & Holliday 2017, 2018). Although there is evidence within their interviews with study abroad students, as they move to subsequent turns, that the people they are talking to are happy to go along with the narratives suggested by the researchers, there must never be complacency about this. On transcribing his interviews with Sara, Adrian began to reflect that he was indeed pushing too hard. For a while, he felt demolished by this discovery and that the whole research event was therefore invalidated. Sara, as a result of her own analysis of the same text, did however point out that she continues to resist and make her resistance known, and therefore finds a way in to research what was going on between them in the interview.

In the next extract we see more of how they negotiate their positionings by referring to a category whose features are well defined and agreed upon by both of them, but whose meanings are brought about inside the conversation from a Centre perspective, and thus commonly shared, not negotiated, and pre-exist the interaction:

Adrian: What was the traveling you've been doing a lot at that time?

Sara: Maybe was more linked to narratives in my family. Because my dad travelled a lot so I've been brought up by listening all those stories of Perù, Colombia, Nigeria, and Iran, he went also to Iran; and I think, and I was surrounded by these narratives and objects also because my parents' house is full of objects that he brought from other places

Adrian: So you had a cosmopolitan upbringing

Sara: Well I don't know if it's cosmopolitan but, of course I had stories coming from other places that were surrounding me

Adrian: Right

Sara: Yes, so I think that that feed- that had fed- fed? Fed yes my curiosity

Adrian: OK that makes sense yes- you told me bits about your father's profession and- but I didn't hear about Colombia and Iran and objects in your home and no- I didn't know about that so so so that's interesting. So you *are* a cosmopolitan person

Sara: (0.5) err well, I don't like definitions anyway

Adrian: OK OK well cosmopolitan isn't a bad definition

Sara: Oh yes, it's a beautiful definition but still I don't know what- yes I don't want to-

We might say that Sara is flirting with what we might refer to as a *positioning categorisation* of being cosmopolitan. On one side she positions herself as associated with being cosmopolitan through reference to the different stories she heard in her childhood about different places. However, soon after this, she refuses the ascription to the positioning categorisation of being cosmopolitan by explaining that she does not like definitions, even though, as she admits in her alignment with Adrian's turn, this is not a bad definition. Sara's projection of a certain identity to her interlocutor here is in fact based on the acknowledgement of a fluid complexity and blurred boundaries, which implies a deCentred refusal of rigid and fixed Centre categories, whether they be national, social or theoretical.

Following on from events in Chapter 2, where the children were sometimes and sometimes not allowing themselves to be positioned in the category of expert travellers, we might say that every 'membership categorisation' (Sacks 1992) entails a certain range of narratives which are shared by the interlocutors but which are also carried into the conversation from outside, so that the co-construction is not of the narrative itself but also of its contextual appropriation. If membership categorisation devices are defined as classifications or social types that may be used to describe persons (Hester & Eglin 1996), we may observe that while positioning negotiations are more in relation to the conversational dynamics and all the narratives and meanings that have arisen in the ongoing event, the membership linked to specific categorisation is built upon external categories that exist in ready-made narratives (cosmopolitan, expert travellers), which precede the interaction and to whom shared meanings and features are given in the process of contextual appropriation. They are therefore shared as part of a more complex and structured Centre grand narrative.

What Sara is doing in the above extract, by partially aligning with, and then distancing herself from, the category of being cosmopolitan, is in a way 'to claim the world as [her] own cultural universe' (Holliday 2011: 61). By doing so, she is actually aligning to the critical cosmopolitan identity that Adrian is suggesting to her, thus *positioning* herself as a cosmopolitan from a deCentred perspective, while not *categorising* herself as a cosmopolitan, as a Centre category.

By following Hester & Hester's (2012: 567) suggestion that 'culture is to be discovered in action', we claim here the relevance of discovering culture through meanings and values given by participants inside small culture formation on the go. This is therefore an invitation not to conceive culture as a Centre *a priori* 'meanings bearer', but to look at how little deCentred actions which challenge Centre established meanings constitute the ongoing process of doing culture, where the concept of culture itself thus should not be the first resource of the analyst but should instead be discovered in what is going on in the interaction itself. This is explained well by Hester & Hester, who suggest that 'it is in their talk-in-interaction (and other social actions) that categories of persons and objects are collected' (567).

Looking at narratives close to us – family background

Family represents a resource of meanings for researchers when they give explanations concerning their engagement with social research. In the next extract, we see how small details concerning family past experiences, practices or events, at a certain point of a story, are mentioned to consolidate reasons and explanations for certain aspects of the cultural journey that the interviewer is presenting. In response to Sara's question about the origins of his researcher professionalism, Adrian returns to his family religious background to explain a personal feature that he presents as a peculiar trait which connects his personal and researcher identity:

Sara: What about professionalism and your ability to do what you are doing in this complex- complicated process of researching and creating identity? How do you manage it?

Adrian: I think I've always wanted to be professional I've always wanted to do things properly ehm and I think this goes back- I mean I've talked to you about this briefly before ehm I've recently been interested in this idea of Protestantism and the reformation which is very much about who you are in juxtaposition with the rest of the world in which you are in so is very much- you be through action. Action is important for being so I've always brought up to- always had to be doing something I was always told off if I said I was bored, always, my mother used to get very angry if I said I was bored you always have to be engaged I always had to be engaged this is what I learnt and I don't enjoy many things unless I'm actively engaged- I mean reading a novel watching a film I have to convince myself that there's a good reason for doing this

'Being active' has thus here the double aim of defining the person *and* the researcher, creating a strong link between the two spheres as if they were feeding each other and presenting the Self as a complex interrelation between different levels that are usually conceived as mutually independent.

This interconnection might become even deeper when narratives involve more or less directly issues related to Centre power, deCentred marginal positions, and the development of critical cosmopolitan perspectives, as can be seen in this email interview response from Nour Elhouda Souleh:[1]

Before I could go to school, I spent a relatively long time with my grandmother; she used to watch me. She strongly believed that nobody is better than anybody. She always told me stories of what the coloniser did to them, and what she had to do during the war to protect my mother and my two uncles. When my elder sister got her baccalaureate degree, my grandmother gave her the French language dictionary

1 Nour is carrying out PhD research at Canterbury Christ Church University on Othering.

'Larousse' as a gift, at that time it was an expensive book to get a hold of. She told her: 'learn their language, and you always be safe'. I think that is what triggered my love for foreign languages.

This narrative strategy to convert a deCentred marginalised positioning into a personal and professional resource is a powerful tool not only within a certain identity construction but also to introduce a third space for alternative narratives.

Of course, Sara's reference to family in the previous extract might be due to Adrian's questions that directly mention upbringing and family background as a suggested explanation for her engagement with research. This can be seen in the next extract. However, it becomes an interviewer choice to read and present small and apparently daily insignificant habits into a meaningful point which can introduce a taste of daily resistance to mainstream laws of belongings. It might, on the other hand, be that, at that time, those moments were just routines with no relevance. It is the act of choosing to describe them now, at the point of analysis, as fundamental bricks in the process of a researcher's life that gives an important political meaning to the whole story. Here we have Sara's response to Adrian, in which, perhaps like Nour, she talks about her family background of discussion despite the fact that 'research' might have been considered an alien concept:

Adrian: You're talking about being inside the university scene ehm- in your upbringing in your family, in your community when you were a child, when you were a teenager was research something which was generally understood and appreciated? Or did it belong to a special group of people?

Sara: No I would say that in my family research was really something far, because my parents and most of my relatives never went to university. It was something that I really discovered about my own person.

Adrian: Is it possible that they could be a more generic form of research? Which isn't part of the university but is to do with how people investigate what's going on around them?

Sara: Yes yes that is something that was really part of my family that's true … I think that for example being critical, learning to be critical, was something that was part of my upbringing because I used to discuss a lot with my parents. We used to have debates about things, about politics; and we used to have also conflicts about ideas so speaking while having dinner, while being all together watching the TV, was something that belongs to me … I don't know if it was different to what other families do. I knew that that was something important in the choices I made and I have made.

What therefore is relevant, when juxtaposing Nour and Sara's accounts of family influence, is how these narratives – besides presenting a connection with the aspect of feeling an outsider that will be discussed below – portray family as a particular kind of resource for the speaker's life and career, which is expressed not in terms of economic and intellectual resources, but, in contrast, as relevant because these families had marginal deCentred positions. As such, these researchers bring into their stories the introduction of a capsising discourse concerning power dynamics and the recognition of the 'unexpected'. What is 'capsising' about this is that, although they do not come from families used to the academic environment, they had other opportunities to develop a critical ability and an observer perspective which they then applied in their academic careers.

Indeed, determination, passion and the 'sweat' of hard work become resources which are independent from economic status and which are learnt in daily practice like watching television for the purpose of self-education, mealtime discussion, writing poems or having books around. This is important because through these personal narratives, participants are presenting an alternative, deCentred story which tries to dismantle the common Centre connection between access to certain social and intellectual environments which imply belonging to higher social classes. Also, as demonstrated in Lalami's telling of the Moor's account in Chapter 1, situated in postcolonial literature, speaking from a pointedly 'non-Western' or 'South' perspective brings an automatic deCentring resource. Here, Nour talks about 'poorness' as not in any way deflecting from 'richness in values', made more poignant by a postcolonial situatedness, that led her to this hard work of self-development, in which even games and deCentring choice of male playmates becomes part:

> I grew up in a very poor family that was rich with its values I would say. I would say that I have learned from my parents to not take a no for an answer, and I had to make it on my own with hard work and sweat. … I used to draw a lot when I was young, but now I cannot remember when was the last time I did it. I think I got from him [her brother] the competitive spirit and love for sports. I played both basketball and volleyball in middle and high school. And I made use of my knowledge and passion for sports in general, and volleyball in particular, to connect with some individuals in my fieldwork.
>
> Both my parents were born during the colonial era with no schooling degrees, still, they insisted that we got ours, and I am very grateful for that. My father could only read the Quran and do simple math equations. My mother had better control of Modern Arabic than he did and she did write some poetry for some time when I was young. I think I might have inherited that from her. I think what influenced me as well

is the books that we had around the house and I read when I was young. I remember when growing up, we had unbelievable loads of books around the house. I never knew where we got them from considering our situation then. The books were mainly about history, Arabic poetry, and literature. I remember when I learned to read, I used to spend hours reading those old books.

Before that, I used to watch a lot of documentaries on TV or try to make sense of those books from whatever pictures in them that I could find. The documentaries were about history (previous civilisations), and freedom fighters from around the world. And, when my mom was not looking I watched a lot Forensic Anatomy shows; the search for the truth always interested me. I would say that by the age of four, I knew everything related to minorities' and colonised countries' fights for freedom and equalities. From the Natives of America, African Americans to Mahatma Ghandi's non-violent approach to peace, you name it. This never crossed my mind before, but I think this is why I am researching what I am researching now.

(Email interview)

Moreover, through these disrupting narratives, participants are creating important cultural threads. It does not matter that we do not know where Nour comes from. There is a mention of language; but the references to colonisation, minorities, class, sport, TV documentaries, a narrative about identity and so on, will resonate with people across the world. This particularity of personal cultural trajectory should help all readers to think of their own particularities in the environments of their upbringing. There is therefore a strong sense of particular cultural trajectory. It is the fact of there *being* a personal cultural trajectory that is important. The thread, therefore, is to enable those of us who read it to think about our own personal cultural trajectories and how they populated our actions.

Although the location of some of these stories might coincide with a cultural 'elsewhere', what they are highlighting is that some processes are created and realised, but also challenged, by and amongst people; and they cannot be ascribed to or justified through artificial pre-constituted national boundaries. They cannot be, therefore, resignedly accepted and taken for granted; but they can be called into question, challenged and re-negotiated in daily discourse and narrative practices.

Dealing with identity dynamics while doing research

These threads also have an effect on the researchers' constructions of belonging itself and the identity aspects linked to it, which are no longer conceptualised in national terms, but are transformed, through these stories, into third spaces.

Here Adrian tells Sara about how he associates his identity with particular histories, places and people, and in so doing seems to be able to step back and also notice, he later states, for the first time, that his identity crosses imagined national boundaries:

Adrian: I am very very attached to a couple of painters and writers who come from Yorkshire and I feel very fond of those people I am quite proud that I share some sort of heritage with them ... but they are much older than me ehm but when I see aspects of their work I can identify with that climate and that city scape and that type of places so I have an identification with that ehm but unusually perhaps I am quite used to other people talking about my identity so ... I guess your identity can to certain extent be something to do with what other people tell you about it and what you read about it so it's not just you who is locating yourself, other people are locating you as well

Sara: So you just answered to my next question cause I wanted to ask you- because so far just before you mentioned this about the relevance of interactions in cultural identity you spoke about your cultural identity as always linked to places, so I wanted to ask you whether it was this the meaning for you of cultural identity, always oriented- linked to places?

Adrian: I had a conversation with one of my students a couple of days ago and she was talking about belonging and ... she said that she was interested in how diverse people's comments about belonging were and it wasn't necessarily to do with where they were born or things like that and it suddenly occurred to me that ... actually I feel a sense of belonging in my students ok? So yes I am pleased that I belong to some sort of interactions with some people I feel a sense of belonging having you as a co-researcher you know, this is something I can belong to, so it doesn't have to be a place, it doesn't have to be a history it could be something that is going on around you that makes you feel as though you belong and it could be quite transient

It is important to observe, with Adrian's thoughtful searching, how these identity construction dynamics are not just something which are academically theorised as if they are external processes which involve anyone but the researcher. Recognising the multidirectional spaces which contribute to the ways the Self is conceptualised and presented becomes a matter which affects researchers personally in their daily lives, and, as such, also the ways they decide to methodologically recognise, bring and consider this issue in their work.

Becoming aware of this critical self-awareness therefore seems to be a skill which needs to be developed and trained in the same way as becoming a good and incisive writer or being capable of grabbing connections between our own theoretical orientations and those who followed similar trajectories before us. In this process of critical self-awareness, there are several elements that the researchers say they have faced and brought into their work. The perception of being an outsider is the one that has more frequently been mentioned and narrated. Another is how the richness of small incidental events are filled with meanings that contribute to self-knowledge and self-reflection. These events are narrated as a sort of epiphany, where personal and researcher are intertwined to light up that process of understanding both ourselves and the Other that is at the very base of the intercultural.

Epiphanies

On some occasions, it is the researcher activities themselves which are described as the turning point through which novice researchers are pushed to reflect also at a personal level and thus to generate urgent but unexpected changes which reverberate in the domains of both the personal and the researcher. In this extract of our interview with Ismatul Zaharin,[2] she talks about how her own views changed quite dramatically in response to her research participants, young university students, undergoing what she refers to as 'radical change':

Sara: What was that you- what have you learnt from engaging with your participants during your PhD research?

Ismatul: Ehm but to be honest the first thing that I learnt from this engagement with my participant I learnt more about interculturality and this question about culture you know and which is what is very related to what I am doing now my research so I learnt more about this I learnt more about- you now when I say culture- cause I used to believe you know when people ask you 'what's your culture' I was saying 'well my culture is so and so' but then- ... but is really not what it is because is- I think is constructed and that's what I was doing when people asked me that question but doing this research it made me realise about all those things you know all these questions about culture how it's actually more than just you know race, nation and things like that

---

2 Ismatul is carrying out PhD research at Canterbury Christ Church University into the cultural identities of undergraduate students.

Sara: How did it happen- I mean what was the time that you realised this- that this change was happening?

Ismatul: It was during my data collection when I started collecting data I asked my participants this one question because I thought like ... I should start with one question and then see where it goes and I started with asking 'how does your intercultural experience of living in the UK affected you?' And I have seven to eight participants and all of them answered differently- talked about different things you know like talked about their changes in appearance, their language how the (...) have changed you know talking about yes different kind of things you know how they've become more spiritual or not things like that so it make me realised about 'ok this intercultural experience or inter-cultural must have something to do more than just culture' because I thought when I asked that question they will say you know like inter-action with this international people (...) but no so yes ...

Adrian: But so what sort of things did you expect them to say?

Ismatul: Well I don't know- I can't remember what I expected initially but I did not expect for them to be talking about- well I do expect that they talked about their changes but then I don't really expect them to reveal so much about their personal inner life here like one of them saying that they were gay you know because- and then why that hap-pened things like that I didn't expect them to talk about that

Sara: So you maybe were thinking more about explanations related to cul-tural differences rather than personal differences? While at the end they gave you more answers concerning personal differences

Ismatul: Yes yes that's right that's right yes

We see here how the interconnection between the personal and the researcher described as the core of changes in Ismatul's life mirrors the interconnections described by her research participants. This shows how the personal bursts unexpectedly into a predefined conception of culture, and is expressed as performative in its manifestation as under construction in the moment of the interview itself.

This observation is important in helping us to understand how the *cul-tural* that we encounter every day is always, in effect, *intercultural*, and the intercultural – which was here the topic that Ismatul aimed to investigate – is a complex process which is fed by, and finds its core in, the interactions amongst people as ongoing travellers not only through countries but also relationships, structures and boundaries of any sort, and life changes.

In Adrian's interview with Sara, she narrates her experience with theatre as a very personal event which had an effect on her researcher sphere. In this extract she identifies a specific moment which is described as a turning point in her pathway, when some activities that took place on the occasion of a theatre workshop became nurturing and inspirational for her engagement in research:

Sara: I can't remember if the notion of researching something was introduced but for example- I remember that one person came- a pretty well-known director in theatre and he worked with us in a workshop where he was using not only text and books but he was using images and he used a very strong painting of Francis Bacon and also some paintings of Hopper and in that moment I started to realise how things are connected- So just by looking at the paintings I was feeling something that have been helping me as actor actress- So yes all these connections I think brought me to understand- to have an idea of research. ... I'm sure that theatre gave me the awareness of this something

What is personally lived, both in terms of personal cultural trajectories and relationships with the people encountered in these journeys, thus becomes an ongoing source of inspiration and reflection – a sort of guide to the observation of social events around us. This is also the case when researchers' narratives include reference to having faced power dynamics. Instead of suppressing researchers, such experiences can become resources at the very outset of research, and indeed be a major impetus of the whole research project. This resilience is not just relevant in researchers' daily acts of realisation during the research process, but its political relevance starts in the very moment of the resilience being narrated. Talmy (2011: 38) suggests that talking about identity is not just talking but *doing* identity. We could say here that talking about resistance and resilience with reference to power dynamics is not just talking, but becomes itself a way of *doing* resistance and resilience. If this becomes empirically realised through research, its performativity becomes even more observable.

Here, Amina Kebabi[3] is quite explicit about how her 'own questioning' arises from moments of outsider interaction with the Other and led to her research trajectory:

It is important to mention that when I noticed and 'sensed' that I am looked at differently because of where I come from, I reacted to this kind of interaction by being 'passive' and neglecting. I was

---

3 Amina is carrying out PhD research into the intercultural identities of university lecturers at Canterbury Christ Church University.

passive and neglecting towards the people I lived with because at the time of this intercultural encounter I believed that it is not my role to make them change the way they think of me and where I come from. Therefore, I believe that my own reaction made these particular people feel that they have the 'authority', or the 'right' to perceive 'me' and 'my culture' the way they did. There was a power dynamics where I was resisting the way the people I lived with were claiming the right to perceive me and 'my culture' the way they did. This is because their reality perception stems from them claiming the truth about viewing me in such a way.

It is clearly shown that as a researcher I am involved in the research process, but in different ways. I am not only researching and generating knowledge from the research participants, but I am also researching myself in terms of where I stand in all of that. How do I make sense of what is being generated from my interaction with the researcher participants? How my own lived experience is going to influence my own understanding of the notion of identity and intercultural encounters and hence, the whole research?

(Email interview)

Here, Amina explains to us how the feeling of being an outsider, or the memory of having felt so at least once in one's life, is strictly linked to these kinds of dynamics. This is an experience which most of the researchers interviewed recalled in their process of giving meanings to their interest in the intercultural and their intercultural journey. Although their experiences of feeling like outsiders might certainly have happened because of Centre-constructed social boundaries and stereotypes, which falsely construct the intercultural as the relationship between members of so-called 'different cultures', and the hierarchical nature of this relationship, these researcher narratives tell us, instead, how these insights into very personal feelings and stories provided a deCentred awareness that allowed them to aspire to a different and more complex understanding of the intercultural.

Being an outsider

These deCentred insights into who is looking at us as Other from them therefore become threads that resist and contest an old, imperialistic, Centre idea of the intercultural. These encounters start at a very early age. Telling these stories, explaining who we are and why we choose to be a certain way, requires time and the willingness to let the Other understand us, and us to understand the Other. It also implies an act of empathy.

Here, Nour speaks again about her 'poorness', and of its impact on her understanding of the world:

> At school, I was not identified as poor nor as rich; I was just different. People did not identify me as poor even though I was considered as one looking back at my family's financial status, and I was not considered rich either because of that. So, my understanding of this sort of 'third space' position that I was in is that because of my high grades I got to be 'different' from the poor, and because of my family's position I could not possibly be rich either. This difference of mine allowed me to know more people from contradicting worlds I would say. I got to see the stereotype that surrounded the poor that the rich had believed in. I got to live the struggles, and to see the inner resilience and the riches that the poor always had, but nobody saw or acknowledged.
>
> (Email interview)

Next to the expression of the feeling of being an outsider in this extract, what is also relevant is that 'being an outsider' it is not just in relation to a majority, an established dominant, Centre category, but to *all* categories. What is narrated is the condition of not belonging, of refusing the adherence to any group and looking for alternative positions – and indeed a third space.

The experience of being an outsider can also be seen in Sara's response in the next extract of her interview with Adrian. She admits how being part of big groups was never easy for her:

Adrian: What happened to you which suddenly put you into this position where you feel less socialised than other people? Because earlier it seems as though you were very happily taking part in everything that was going on even when you started the drama group you were just going along with the others

Sara: Yes but it was- no I didn't say it was easier because I had moments in which I was feeling alone and I still have moments as I had- maybe now I know better how to manage them but moments in which I feel a bit lost when I am surrounded by too many people and- mm like as if some dynamics were clear to everybody but me

Adrian: What's your earliest feeling of that?

Sara: I think when I was in primary school- no I was- it was the moment of the three years you have soon after the primary school, which is called here 1st grade secondary school and I had- I think that was the moment- yes because I was like playing soccer with all the males of the classroom and for this reason ((laughs)) I was a little bit like outside- an outsider for the girls' group and so I wasn't-

Adrian: Why did you want to play soccer?
Sara: Well, I liked ((laughs))- because I liked that
Adrian: Where did that come from?
Sara: I don't know- maybe because I grew up with my cousins they were all males and they were like playing with me and I was more used to- I was used to play with males I think- with boys

In everyday life interactions, the idea of taking up deCentred positions does not concern thus the kind of group a person decides to adhere to. It is not a matter of dichotomies between good and bad, majority or minority, or boys or girls. It is rather the narrative power of adopting unexpected deCentred positions that are able to break expectations related to the common forms of belonging. Taking up a deCentred position has more to do with how we decide to look at and approach dominant categories rather than which category we adhere to. While the second option, even when adopting a marginal position, would imply a reconfirmation and reproduction of existing boundaries, the first option performs a deconstruction of these boundaries and, by so doing, moves beyond them.

This becomes evident in the above extract where Sara is cutting across the two dominant categories of 'boys' and 'girls' by referring to personal taste – 'Well, I liked ((laughs))- because I liked that'. Her movement between the two groups is thus not legitimated by any form of social expectation or strategy. It is instead grounded in a personal choice and attitude which does not have a correspondence with an easy polarisation of masculine or feminine behaviour.

As Sara admits in a later interview:

Sara: It also leads to the feeling that I still recognise and I still- and I remember very well of not feeling belong- of not feeling any kind of belonging.

A girl playing soccer with boys, and talking about this as a meaningful aspect of self-reflection about identity, therefore does not mean seeing oneself belonging to one group instead of another, but instead to question established categories and dominant expectations by giving space and recognition to deCentred positionings and thus challenging dominant narratives. This is the way in which deCentredness can be conceived: not as a deCentred position compared to a Centred one, but rather a positioning choice which brings a particular narrative – to look at things from or give space to an alternative, unexpected, troublesome perspective. This feeling and this narrative choice recur in other interviews. Here, Nour talks again about how being Othered in her childhood – also regarding 'boy' and 'girl' groups – becomes an opportunity:

> Growing up, especially in high school, I had more male friends than female ones. For some reason, girls never liked me. Surprise! Surprise! Surprise! I remember that they refused to sit next to me in the classroom. So, I always end up sitting next a boy or to some girl from a poor background like myself. But, I learned to make the best out of every situation. And, that helped me a lot to connect with the male individuals that I was working with at my workplace. In the female department though, I was *not* so popular; I was called: 'Boya' which means a girl that is like a boy.
>
> I've got an internal self which is not social at all which is just me and the universe and in which I feel I'm absolutely totally alone.
>
> (Email interview)

Although, in this extract, belonging to one group excludes the possibility of belonging to another one, the focus of the account here is about the learning process that this experience gave to the researcher, as a kind of awareness to draw from. We therefore surmise that this awareness concerning the take-up of deCentred positions makes it easier for researchers to apply the important ethnographic discipline of making the familiar strange. It is the experience of outsiderness and a certain level of detachment which can provide a measured and observant sensitivity that enables some researchers to keep their eyes trained to look at the deCentred aspects of social interactions.

Handling doubts and uncertainties with narrative

We have seen in the interviews in this chapter a relationship between an observant, reflexive sensitivity about who we are and an observant sensitivity about the lives of others that helps to dissolve Centre boundaries. If, concerning ourselves, we are aware of limits about what we want to share and, mostly, of how to use it in our behaviour as researchers, what are the boundaries that need to be respected when we manage what has been revealed to us?

Reflections concerning professional responsibility as researchers are strictly twined with the other topics which we have considered to be part of researchers' narratives; and, most importantly, they are embedded in the action of taking up deCentred positionings. The reason for this deep connection is that recognising Otherness and building third spaces, where the plays on these positionings and explorations become possible, requires an acknowledgement of the political implications behind this action. Whether in the person we are communicating with or ourselves, the creation of third spaces and the act of taking up deCentred positionings cannot help but require an ethical and moral rigour with regard to the political power that this implies.

It is because of the multiple meanings that Otherness brings with itself, that handling it requires the professional ability to recognise that every choice we make with data is a choice which implies an effect on how the world is constructed and what meanings are conveyed. Sara talks about her responsibility in this regard in her interview with Adrian:

Sara: So, what I really hope is to be able to catch those things that the people I'm interviewing really think are important to be said; and I really care to make them accessible also to other people. And then maybe sometimes they hope that by telling me these things, things might change. So, this is something that I really hope to be able to- to do in research. But at the same time I found myself sometimes- and I am still finding myself worrying about their privacy. So worrying that the things that I decide to speak about and to reveal during my research and report, they might bring these people to be recognised in a way or to make a damage to them. … But also more in general. I mean when you have a story, the story of a person it's a big gift that that person gives to you, you know, telling you her or his story. And sometimes these stories are so deep and so rich that for me is- I feel that it's a big responsibility to manage that with- really, with care. Not that I don't manage with care also the others, you know, but it's also how people that will read my work, how do they really interpret those words. Am I able to really- to explain things in a proper way so that everyone will see the same. I mean it's impossible- so this scares me a bit.

The kind of worry that she expresses here is an aspect which is cutting across all the interviews; and we can thus claim that it populates researchers' narratives generally.

Understanding this sense of responsibility represents an important aspect of how doubts and uncertainties are handled by creating a third space in which uncertainties and doubts become resources and not dangerous elements to get rid of. This is a task and a purpose concerning the meanings that we construct in the whole experience of doing research. This is shown well in the next extract from our interview with Ismatul. Here, she explains how she begins to understand, through trying to be faithful to what the young people she is researching are telling her, the constructed nature of culture. She refers to the courage it takes to step out of the normal way of talking about herself and others:

Ismatul: I think so yes it actually change my whole perspective about you know like individuals you know like err I should- like think about other people as an individual you know try not to stereotype or try not to categorise a group … you know because ehm yes because that's also what I feel about myself now because previously- like what I told you- I thought when people ask me to talk about my culture I talked about what- you know me being Malaysian like Malay but then I realised what I have been telling people is not really something that personally related to me- is something- is just something that is socially constructed so yes but now I think I've changed

Adrian: So you also talked to other people about more personal things than about constructed cultural things?

Ismatul: I guess so yes, yes yes

Sara: I am thinking that this is also an act of courage in a way because of course it's easier to tell people stereotypes about the place you come from because it's easier in a way you just stay on a very superficial level while entering in a deep personal description is of course harder in a way I think so I was thinking while you were saying this yes about me and when I am doing this and when I am not and yes- are you always doing this or sometimes you still find yourself going back to a stereotyped- because- but now in an aware- with awareness

Ismatul: Yes yes especially when talking about myself I would say that- you know because sometimes like you said when we talk to someone you've just met you don't want to reveal so much you know and plus you try to cut the conversation short cause you know you don't want to be like talking all the times and maybe people are not interested to listen to you but then- so sometimes it would probably be easier to just like do that but … I tried not to do that much and try not to- like you saw- like these stereotypes things- yes because I think I've personally changed because I- I- even in my like personal life I don't like to do that anymore you know like- I always try to think more deeply when I look at something or someone 'oh probably she's doing this because of this or because of this' you know I try not to- yes sort of categorise them yes

Sara: Yes

Adrian: Does that make it harder?

Ismatul: Ehm I don't think is harder for me cause I am quite used to it now but is harder when I have to discuss about you know like someone or something with another person who is not thinking the same way as- for instance when I am talking to … my husband it's quite hard sometime you know because I always try not to judge people so I say 'maybe it's like this because maybe she's doing this because of this' and he will be like 'no nonono I don't think so you know I think like that' so it's quite hard

This extract is important in that it brings together a number of themes in this chapter. Ismatul's reference to the joint production of a narrative, for instance, represents a description of how several people create small culture on the go and find themselves together working out rules for engagement ('because sometimes like you said when we talk to someone you've just met you don't want to reveal so much you know and plus you try to cut the conversation short cause you know you don't want to be like talking all the times and maybe people are not interested to listen to you but then'). In this process, we can recognise a substratum of previous shared codes and knowledge which bring us to share a certain language and to choose certain words to make our thoughts more comprehensible to the other people we are involved with. Here, Ismatul is positioning herself with the young people she is researching and, through them, gains a new understanding that the dominant narrative of the large culture that she has always associated herself with is socially constructed: 'I think I've personally changed because I- I-even in my like personal life I don't like to do that anymore you know like- I always try to think more deeply when I look at something or someone'.

Secondly, the interconnection between professional researcher choices and personal changes is an important topic upon which the narratives are built. It has the relevant aim not only to define the researcher's identity but also to reconfirm their professional group and its legitimation, which develops around the use of certain words and the adherence to certain theoretical approaches (marked in italics in the extract). It is through the expression of and negotiation around a certain *Weltanschauung* that every small culture legitimates and reproduces itself, by creating boundaries of adherence and sparks of differentiation to the rest of the world ('another person who is not thinking the same way as-').

A third aspect is the creation of a third space – a space in which not having answers is possible and investigated. In this sense, Ismatul is finding another, initially uncomfortable and courageous place from which to look at the people she is researching, and from which they themselves require her to do so because of their own deCentred behaviour. She is also having to deCentre her own viewpoint to be able to understand their deCentredness ('I always try to think more deeply when I look at something or someone 'oh probably she's doing this because of this or because of this' you know I try not to- yes sort of categorise them yes').

In this together

In this chapter we have looked in some detail at how researchers themselves talk about their own positioning and narratives. In many ways they speak about themselves in similar ways to the people that they study as research 'participants'. This reminds us that we are all 'participants' in the research that we carry out – confirming its co-constructed nature as discussed in Chapter 1. Not that this is different to many people; it is noticeable that the researchers in this chapter are also cultural travellers who experience discordance and have personal narratives about family and childhood. This resonates with the idea that our interculturality goes back to our early experience. They all also speak about greater or lesser degrees of deCentredness that come from being outsiders in some aspects of their lives, including sometimes in childhood, which in turn makes them work hard at the Self-Other identity politics of positioning. Like the children with migration backgrounds in Chapter 2, they also have it high on their agendas to resist or not resist how they are positioned by others – hence the threads we have with the children not being what we expect. There is therefore a shared contextualisation of doubts and uncertainties, of being pushed and pulled by life interactions and the epiphanies of a group of people who are not easily or automatically socialised. These researchers are unsure participants in small culture formation on the go who co-construct deCentred third spaces. However, this image of the unsure, uncertain researcher who is brought up with outsider deCentred experience does not mean directionless confusion. We feel that it is this quality that enables researchers to achieve the 'comprehension of the conditions and often complex processes in which people are caught up' which 'transcends one's status as Insider or Outsider' (Merton, R. K. 1972: 41).

5   Getting on with deCentred life

In this concluding chapter we will present the final and unexpected discovery of a non-essentialist, deCentred 'getting on with life' grand narrative, and, in so doing, pull together the overall message of the book. We introduced this narrative briefly in Chapter 1 and feel it an important place to finish because it breaks the common presumption that all grand narratives are Centred and essentialist. Its discovery thus takes us into a major third space and reveals the possibility of deCentred threads of a larger magnitude than we might have imagined possible. The discovery of the deCentred grand narrative emerges from an interaction between a teacher and students that itself takes the form of an unexpected third space. Calling it a 'discovery' might sound dramatic; but discoveries in social research are perhaps inevitable once the very difficult task of negotiating out of Centre thinking is somehow achieved.

Meeting undergraduate students

The discovery event is reconstructed in the following ethnographic account about the continued experience of Kati while teaching undergraduate students and her conversations about it with her friends, Eli and Matt.[1]

> While she was doing her masters course in intercultural communication, Kati had the opportunity to teach a group of undergraduate students from the Media Department. From the beginning, she found it difficult to create a rapport with them. She had been told that she could do what she liked as long as it was relevant to the part of the syllabus

---

1 This reconstructed ethnographic account is based on our own experience of teaching undergraduate students and its resonances with research in which the cultural realities of students are often not able to express themselves because of the structures of educational systems (Canagarajah 2004), as previously referred to in Chapter 2.

entitled 'Migration'. They'd been receiving lectures on the topic; and, with her, a smaller group was supposed to have open discussion seminars. The programme director seemed quite decent and told her that her 'background in culture' should be an important contribution.

She had taught before in her own country, so wasn't too nervous. It was the first time for her to teach in English, which was an optional language for the students to choose for the seminar; but this didn't worry her. It was her normal language for study, as the course she was doing was English-medium; and the students seemed also to have no problem with it. However, they didn't seem overly interested in 'migration'. She showed them extracts of texts and images on PowerPoint and asking them to comment. They had little to say. She began to wonder if it was possible for young people not really to connect with the issues even though there was immense discussion about migration throughout the media. Although they lived in a country into which considerable migration was taking place, and where disturbing images were now commonplace on television news, she felt that it didn't really seem to have touched them. She was also surprised because when she was their age she considered herself an activist regarding her own government's policies on human rights.

Kati also wondered if their reticence was something to do with her teaching style. She decided to get some advice. Although the programme director had said he was there to be consulted if needed, she wasn't sure he'd be sympathetic. She felt he was like her teachers on the masters course who thought that it was *she* who 'lacked criticality' because of her 'culture'. She therefore wasn't sure how he would react to *her* suggesting that *his* students, from *his* 'culture', weren't being actively critical. It might also sound as though she was critiquing his teaching in the lecture part of the course.

So she decided to talk to Matt. Even though she, him and Eli had had disagreements about their field trip to the 'migrant' suburb, they all found it useful to share and discuss. He was their 'local' informant, while she and Eli thought that they were his 'token', 'other culture' friends. However, when Matt said that the students might be finding her approach difficult because she was trying to get them to talk about people who came from different cultures when she herself was also from a different culture, Kati felt that he really was going too far. However, when she told Eli what he said, Eli thought there was some truth in it. Eli thought that the students behaviour might be an example of how Westerners isolate foreigners with a wall of apparently polite but deeply patronising silence. Eli then said that Kati needed to come at the whole thing from a completely different direction by not talking about migration at all because it just frightened everyone and brought out the worst in them – superficial well-wishing or blatant racism. Eli said that Kati should try to introduce a different type of thinking to catch the students unawares so that their racism wasn't activated.

While Kati found Matt's sustained essentialism annoying, she could now see that it might be possible that at least some of the students might be thinking in the way he suggested and that, while Eli's suggestion was also a bit essentialist, the idea of coming at things differently did seem right.

It becomes evident here that negotiating classroom content and teaching style can lay bare a number of positions and their attendant narratives. Perhaps the most important for Kati as a novice teacher is her unspoken but deeply felt views about what her programme director might think if she approached him with her problem. There is in Kati's mind a conflict between the values about criticality that she brings with her and the values that she feels she is expected to have in the society that she has travelled to. Of course, because she does not speak out, it is not known what the response of the programme director would be. Eli's response to what Matt says about the students probably being silent because of cultural difference, that the silence of Westerners is their mode of disapproval, might be an 'over the top' over-interpretation. However, it comes from what Eli has observed elsewhere. Whether or not her 'West versus the rest' narrative is an appropriate labelling for the locations of her cultural travel, Eli perceives and has indeed felt a Centre-deCentred politics to do with silence. There has been much written about the silence of the disenfranchised as resistance – biding time during hopelessness until there is the possibility that speaking out will make a difference.[2] This certainly resonates with our recent experience of interviewing a visiting student who is in conflict with the owner of her accommodation. She tells us what is in her mind during the conflict, but did not speak it at the time the conflict took place (Amadasi & Holliday 2018: 249).

Another unexpected deCentred thread

In a sense, therefore, this Centre-deCentre politics between Kati and her colleagues and friends is already setting the scene for what happens in the

2 Discussions of silence as an expression of resistance can be found in Flam and Bauzamy (2008) and Sawyer and Jones (2008: 245, citing Scott). This process has also been referred to as 'strategic essentialism' – a term that has often been attributed to Gayatri Spivak (Danius & Jonsson 1993). See also Holliday's discussion of strategic discoursal withdrawal (2011: 179–180, 2018c: 94).

classroom. In particular, thinking in these terms provides a discoursal layering that heightens Kati's criticality even further and perhaps makes her more confident to innovate – perhaps influencing her choice of the deCentred material she uses and helping her to recognise what she finds:

In the next class, Kati played the TED lecture by the Nigerian writer Chimamanda Ngozi Adichie, 'The Danger of a Single Story'.[3] Somehow, she felt, it seemed to connect with the students. She couldn't quite work out why. Perhaps it was because it was a different medium to what she'd tried before. Perhaps it was the power with which Adichie spoke. Perhaps it was because she spoke about something more personal. The video had been discussed in Kati's intercultural communication class as an example of a different approach to developing intercultural awareness.[4] Kati liked it because it really resonated with her own experience – Adichie talking passionately about how where she came from was so little talked about in the West that the complexity was rarely appreciated, and that there were so many stories about Nigerians and people like them that were often not heard. From what some of the students said, it seemed that this lack of recognition also resonated with their experience as teenagers who are so often misunderstood by their parents and other adults.

Whatever it was, there was quite a discussion; and several of the students asked her if she knew about a song that many of them liked called 'No Roots'.[5] Kati didn't know the song at all; so they explained to her that it speaks about growing up travelling frequently without roots. They asked her if they could discuss the lyrics in class. Therefore, Kati found the song on the internet and took the lyrics to the next class to analyse with the students.

During the class, Kati did note that some students were absent. Others said that they weren't there because they didn't want to discuss the song but that she shouldn't worry about it as they had the right to choose. Kati drew attention to several key phrases in the lyrics. She said that the idea of travelling 'like gypsies in the night' seemed very

---

3 This lecture (Adichie 2009) can be found at www.ted.com/talks/chimamanda_adichie_the _danger_of_a_single_story?language=en

4 'The Danger of a Single Story' lecture is used in the IEREST intercultural awareness course for Erasmus students moving to different cultural environments across Europe (Beaven & Borghetti 2015: 13) referred to in Chapter 3.

5 A version of this song (Merton, A. & Rebcher 2017) can be found at www.songtexte.com/ songtext/alice-merton/no-roots-g7bceeedc.html, where it is performed by one of the writers, Alice Merton.

poetic and nostalgic. She shared with them how it made her remember images in Mahmudan Hawad's *Caravane de la soif*,[6] which had been imprinted on her mind many years before when she read it as an undergraduate student at home. Some of the students seemed to like her talking about her own experience of being a student like them. Also, they discussed how having memories contributed to journeys being positive elements in the singer's cultural identity. Finally, Kati suggested that having no roots, but still having a home which is differently conceived of as somewhere which is not on the ground, was itself an identity statement – a declaration of proud diversity in contrast to how things are usually conceived to be.

Kati felt so inspired by finding herself developing these ideas with the students on the basis of something that they had unexpectedly suggested to her. Some students said they thought that the song presented a negative description of being a frequent traveller. Others, who said that they were the 'more romantic group', thought it was a positive description of this condition. Kati joined their discussion and said she felt that she was part of the 'romantic group'. Then they asked her to play the song on YouTube so they could watch it being performed together.

Then, while Kati was still trying to make sense of the polarised, positive and negative interpretations that the students had suggested, there was a new interpretation that seemed to come from the whole group. This was that there was a third, new, wider meaning, which cut across this polarisation. This was that the singer was making a statement concerning her *own* identity – that she was not saying whether this way of growing up amongst frequent geographical movement was good or not, but just saying 'this is the way I am'.

Kati was so impressed and excited that she shared the experience of the students and the song with Eli. She didn't go to Matt because she thought that he really wouldn't understand at all. It took Eli a while to get the implication; but then she came up with an interesting idea – that what the students were talking about was some sort of different way of thinking about things that was somehow independent of all the politics of migration and cultural difference. Eli said that on her course they had been talking about different grand narratives in history and the present day – the big stories that politicians and countries use to influence identity. She said that these stories seemed usually to be so divisive

6 Images from this book (Hawad 1987) can be found at www.google.co.uk/search?q=Cara vane+de+la+soif&client=safari&hl=en-gb&prmd=svin&source=lnms&tbm=isch&sa=X& ved=0ahUKEwit_eP5s8bdAhVKJ8AKHWnlBhkQ_AUIEygD&biw=768&bih=954#imgrc =tfen8LIWfbTcpM

and even the cause of wars, revolutions and terrorism, but that the song might represent a grand narrative that did not do that.

Kati knew all about divisive grand narratives. The history of her country was littered with them – mostly completely untrue. It was also a grand narrative that the West had about the rest of the world, that was derived from colonialism, that led their tutors to think of Eli and her as uncivilised groupies who couldn't think for themselves. Despite her excitement about the discussion with the students, she had noted in the way that some of them had looked at her when she mentioned the Hawad book, that they were surprised that she had learnt anything before she came for education in their country.

Kati was therefore all the more inspired by the thought that these students, despite being caught within the same grand narrative about foreigners as their teachers, had just possibly expressed some sort of 'getting on with life' grand narrative that instead deals with complexity and diversity and the best of humanity. Eli said that it reminded her of something she had read about being 'deCentred' and 'hybrid'.

When they talked to Matt about it, he also seemed to know what they were getting at and said it was to do with Stuart Hall talking about the margins. Eli just looked at him as though someone like him could never begin to understand what Stuart Hall was about. Kati, though, thought that Eli was being too hard on him when he said that this new grand narrative related to something he had noticed about the behaviour of people after a recent terrorist attack. She could see that Eli was about to get at him for using the word 'terrorist' so easily and motioned to her to listen. He said that after the attack, there were so many people from all sorts of backgrounds that saw past their differences and came together to help each other.

This, she thought, was exactly what this new narrative of basic humanity was about. It is what keeps us all going. Kati thought that this 'getting on with life' *was* a grand narrative, but of a different type. It came from the sides and bypassed the type driven by politicians and divisive ideas of nation. She thought it might be populated by unprejudiced personal narratives of all types.

At the obvious level, this account shows the construction of a *modus operandi* between Kati and her students. It is however also a deep and unexpected discovery of multiple deCentred threads within a small culture formation on the go of shifting and competing narratives and positionings.

Although the students are 'Western', the ones that stay seem to take well to the Adichie lecture. Then, quite independently of their teacher, they relate it to the 'No Roots' song, which might also be labelled as deCentred.

Adichie's lecture is deCentred by design in that it is speaking explicitly from the margins about how the Centre's stereotypical imagination of people like her is Othering in its reductive simplicity. The song, however, we wish to frame as *unexpectedly* deCentred because it comes from the students themselves, even though some of them may be positioning Kati as an uncivilised foreigner and it is written and performed by people who might also be framed as Westerners.[7] It is beyond the scope of this book to discuss the musicology of the song. What is important to note here is that it may well speak to the students' own personal experiences of being deCentred as teenagers seeking identity. This resonates with the deCentred feelings of the researchers about their own upbringings in Chapter 4. The song then speaks back to Kati and resonates with her memory of another, to her, deCentred text – that of *Caravane de la soif.* Kati's reference to this text then resonates with the students because she is sharing her own undergraduate student experience.

Connecting back to other events

The account of Kati's experience with the students also takes in her continued small culture formation on the go with her friends, Eli and Matt. They each also shift their positions and narratives, not just in terms of the new narrative that is talked about explicitly in the classroom, but in terms of the ones expressed by each person as they arrive at their understanding of what might be going on. Matt seems to suffer quite a lot in this account in that he provides what Kati considers to be quite an essentialist analysis of why the students do not initially respond to what Kati is trying to do – to her falsely suggesting that it is because of their perception of Kati as coming from another culture. This resonates for her with how he reacted to the 'migrant suburb' in Chapter 3, and, for Kati, how he initially reacts to the woman on the train in Chapter 1. Even though Matt has a background in cultural studies and was initially quite careful about the politics of labelling, he revealed his essentialist views about what he considered a 'backward' culture and the woman's 'collectivist' cultural deficiency. His problem might be that although he has been to classes and heard about the theory, and he makes the connection with Stuart Hall, he has never been challenged. One might say that people who only know the Centre never understand. However, Matt might well have had deCentred life experience, but needs to be able to find it. We see this beginning to happen as he struggles to find a deCentred third

---

7 The songwriters are British-German and German; and the record company is German.

space in his making sense of the woman on the train. In this respect, he is beginning to find what the researchers in Chapter 4 also express.

Kati however changes her mind when Eli unexpectedly agrees with Matt; and it is his interpretation that is instrumental in bringing her to a solution of what to do.

This finding of the deCentred in ourselves no matter where we come from is perhaps at the heart of interculturality. Thinking in these terms is in a sense at the very core of any sort of intercultural understanding. In effect, whatever narratives were initially preventing the students connecting with Kati, it was her eventually presenting them with something deCentred, in Adichie's video, that cut through the narratives and created a thread that enabled them to present a deCentred thread from their own experience back again.

Of course, we never know exactly what is going on. It may be that the students in the initial session *were* connecting silently with what Kati was doing, and that it just took time until the next session for them to express the connection. It may also be the case that they themselves did not think that they were connecting when tacitly they were – which set the unconscious ground-work for the explicit thread to emerge later. It may also be the case that the students who left might years later remember and find a significant thread with the event long past. It is also significant that the students named the grouping that engaged with Kati 'the more romantic group', which Kati is then herself able to find a thread with. This is the act of naming a narrative so that we can position ourselves with or against it.

Conclusions

To conclude, we revisit the main theme of this book – finding deCentred threads. Small culture formation on the go has been the environment where the search has taken place – the space in which we engage with or pass by each other and where the everyday intercultural takes place, whether travelling huge cultural distances or interacting with the more familiar. In this shifting and often discordant environment, deCentring is made possible in uncomfortable third spaces. We see this throughout the events in each chapter, from the extreme circumstances in *The Moor's Account* in Chapter 1, to we researchers interviewing each other in Chapter 4. In these cases, a third space is found and deCentring takes place where the normal is disturbed and we become aware of Centre structures and work to put them aside or work around them. These are the circumstances for deCentred threads to be formed.

In Chapter 3 it also becomes clear that threads – the resonances that dissolve Centre boundaries and bring us together – are themselves complex and may not be what they seem, and might in some circumstances result in essentialist Centre blocks. In small culture formation on the go, people may also be seduced by essentialist Centre grand narratives that turn apparent resonance into blocks instead of threads. Kati thus becomes aware that her apparent threads with Eli are based upon essentialising others. This struggle for threads is itself a consequence of the discomfort of third spaces, which are often fraught by diverse and often competing narratives and positioning. A major turning point in the book is where, in Chapter 2, Sara chooses to create a space which encourages threads with primary school children. However, this results in the children's play with narratives, some of which resist the positionings she suggests. Understanding this resistance is instrumental in unseating the Centre narrative that falsely characterises the children as always being essentially culturally confused. We are not suggesting that cultural confusion in itself is a bad thing, especially given that we researchers often find ourselves culturally confused as we enter third spaces. The children may or may not be culturally confused at different times and for different reasons. There is also a 'reality' in the fact that they are constructed by others as culturally confused. What we are arguing in this book is that such a construction must never be applied to a particular group of people as though it is an essential part of who they are as members of a particular large culture or as having experienced migration. The final thread that emerges from Sara's necessarily sustained intervention is not quite where she initially thought it would be. Something similar happens to Kati working with undergraduate students at the beginning of this chapter. What this means is that seeking to create threads opens up opportunities for unexpected threads to emerge on their own terms which are themselves difficult.

'On their own terms' is a headline phrase for the marginalised to 'come into representation', as we learn from Stuart Hall in Chapter 1. There is no other way if we are to see people differently to how they are defined by the Centre. It is these deCentred descriptions of who we all are to which threads need to relate. Therefore, it was only when, as a result of beginning threads, and then sustained efforts to get them right, that the children in Chapter 2 and the students in this chapter gained space to express themselves and their personal views so that the threads could begin to work, and, in the case of the students, for the totally unexpected 'getting on with life' grand narrative to emerge.

The constructivist research methodology is also central to this struggle to understand. Discarding the false security of large culture structures that define 'the differences between' and place third spaces 'in-between' them, has required diverse methods and settings to get to the bottom of the complex of intertwining narratives and positioning. Interviewing ourselves and other researchers in Chapter 4 helped us to understand more deeply how we researchers join with the people in our studies to make mutual sense of the Centre, of prejudice, and of how we need to engage to bring the deCentred to the surface so that threads can be constructed. Being open about our own struggles as researchers is in itself crucial for us to enter into third spaces. Small culture formation on the go is not therefore just the spaces where the people we watch work out their blocks and threads; it also where we researchers work out our own blocks and threads, with them and with each other.

While what we describe in this book are the social dynamics that take place on a daily basis throughout our lives, there are Centre structures that can make it difficult for us to appreciate them as such. These social dynamics present a complexity and diversity which take enormous awareness and observational ability to appreciate because they run against established Centre discourses and narratives. This tension between what is going on and what the Centre tells us is going on can bring about an instinctive reaction of fear and dismay as we attempt to find answers which are complicated and sometimes impossible. We have tried hard to represent what is going on without falling too much into the traps of easy Centre equations and formulae – trying to give solutions, while at the same time knowing our inability to face and accept the unpredictability of social life.

Bibliography

Adichie, C. N. (2009). The danger of a single story. *TED Lectures*. http://www.ted. com/talks/chimamanda_adichie_the_danger_of_a_single_story?language=en

Agar, M. (1990). Text and fieldwork: 'exploring the excluded middle'. *Journal of contemporary ethnography* 19, 1, 73–88.

Amadasi, S. (2016). Children and transnational identities in the context of compulsory schooling. Methodological notes from research conducted in Parma and Reggio Emilia/Italy. In Maier-Höfer, C. (Ed.), *Angewandte Kindheitswissenschaften: Eine Einführung in das Paradigma*, 209–232. Springer.

Amadasi, S. & Holliday, A. R. (2017). Block and thread intercultural narratives and positioning: conversations with newly arrived postgraduate students. *Language Intercultural Communication* 17, 3, 254–269.

Amadasi, S. & Holliday, A. R. (2018). 'I already have a culture.' Negotiating competing grand and personal narratives in interview conversations with new study abroad arrivals. *Language & Intercultural Communication* 18, 12, 241–256.

Amadasi, S. & Iervese, V. (2018). The right to be transnational. Narratives and Positionings of children with migration background in Italy. In Baraldi, C. & Cockburn, T. (Eds.), *Theorizing childhood: citizenship, rights and participation*, 239–262. Palgrave Macmillan.

Baraldi, C. (2009). Empowering dialogue in intercultural settings. In Baraldi, C. (Ed.), *Dialogue in intercultural communities: from an educational point of view*, 3–28. John Benjamins.

Baraldi, C. (2014a). *Facilitare la comunicazione in classe. Suggerimenti dalla metodologia della narrazione e della riflessione*. FrancoAngeli.

Baraldi, C. (2014b). Promotion of migrant children's epistemic status and authority in early school life. *International Journal of Early Childhood* 47, 5–25.

Barker, C. & Galasiński, D. (2001). *Cultural studies and discourse analysis: a dialogue on language and identity*. Routledge.

Baumann, G. (1996). *Contesting culture*. Cambridge University Press.

Beaven, A. & Borghetti, C. (2015). *Intercultural education resources for Erasmus students and their teachers*. University of Primorska, Annales University Press.

Beck, U. & Sznaider, N. (2006). Unpacking cosmopolitanism for the social sciences: a research agenda. *British Journal of Sociology* 57, 1, 1–23.

Berger, P. & Luckmann, T. (1979). *The social construction of reality*. Penguin.

Bhabha, H. K. (1994). *The location of culture*. Routledge.

Blackman, S. J. (2000a). 'Decanonised knowledge' and the radical project: towards an understanding of cultural studies in British universities. *Pedagogy, Culture & Society* 8, 1, 43–67.

Blackman, S. J. (2000b). 'Decanonised knowledge' and the radical project: towards an understanding of cultural studies in British universities. *Pedagogy, Culture & Society* 8, 1, 43–67.

Borghetti, C. & Beaven, A. (2018). Monitoring class interaction to maximise intercultural learning in mobility contexts. In Jackson, J. & Oguro, S. (Eds.), *Intercultural interventions in study abroad*, 53–77. Routledge.

Botting, F. (1995). Culture, subjectivity and the real; or, psychoanalysis reading postmodernity. In Adam, B. & Allan, S. (Eds.), *Theorising culture: an interdisciplinary critique after postmodernism*, 87–99. UCL Press.

Butterworth, J., Butterworth, T. & Richardson, J. (2018). *Britannia*. Sky.

Canagarajah, A. S. (2004). Subversive identities, pedagogical safe houses, and critical learning. In Norton, B. & Toohey, K. (Eds.), *Critical pedagogies and language learning*, 96–116. Cambridge University Press.

Clifford, J. (1986). Introduction: partial truths. In Clifford, J. & Marcus, G. E. (Eds.), *Writing culture: the poetica of politics of ethnography*, 1–26. University of California Press.

Clifford, J. & Marcus, G. E. (Eds.) (1986). *Writing culture: the poetics and politics of ethnography*. University of California Press.

Cohen, L. (1992). Anthem. On *The future*. Columbia.

Collins, H. (2017). Interculturality from above and below: navigating uneven discourses in a neoliberal university system. *Language & Intercultural Communication* 18, 2, 1–17.

Cribb, A. & Gewirtz, S. (2013). The hollowed-out university? A critical analysis of changing institutional and academic norms in UK higher education. *Discourse: Studies in the Cultural Politics of Education* 34, 3, 338–350.

Crown, S. (2015). The Moor's Account by Laila Lalami review – a story with extraordinary power. *The Guardian*. https://www.theguardian.com/books/2015/aug/20/the-moors-account-laila-lalami-review?CMP=Share_iOSApp_Other

Danius, S. & Jonsson, S. (1993). An interview with Gayatri Chakravorty Spivak. *Boundary* 20, 2, 24–50.

Davis, A. (2017). *Revolution today*. CCCB, Centre de Cultura Contemporarània de Barcelona.

Delanty, G. (2006). The cosmopolitan imagination: critical cosmopolitanism and social theory. *British Journal of Sociology* 57, 1, 25–47.

Delanty, G., Wodak, R. & Jones, P. (Eds.) (2008). *Identity, belonging and migration*. Liverpool University Press.

Dervin, F. (2011). A plea for change in research on intercultural discourses: A 'liquid' approach to the study of the acculturation of Chinese students. *Journal of Multicultural Discourses* 6, 1, 37–52.

Dervin, F. (2016). *Interculturality in education*. Palgrave Macmillan.

Durkheim, E. (1952). *Suicide: a study in sociology*. Routledge & Kegan Paul.

Fairclough, N. (1995). *Critical discourse analysis: the critical study of language*. Addison Wesley Longman.

Fairclough, N. (2006). *Language and globalization*. Routledge.

Flam, H. & Bauzamy, B. (2008). Symbolic violence. In Delanty, G., Wodak, R. & Jones, P. (Eds.), *Identity, belonging and migration*, 221–240. Liverpool University Press.

Gafaranga, J. (2001). Linguistic identities in talk-in-interaction order in bilingual conversation. *Joumal of Pragmatics* 33, 1901–1925.

Giddens, A. (1984). *The constitution of society*. Polity Press.

Goffman, E. (1959). *The presentation of self in everyday life*. Doubleday.

Gong, Y. & Holliday, A. R. (2013). Cultures of change. In Hyland, K. & Wong, L. (Eds.), *Innovation and change in English language education*, 44–57. Routledge.

Goodson, I. (2006). The rise of the life narrative. *Teacher Education Quarterly* 33, 4, 7–21.

Guilherme, M. (2002). *Critical citizens for an intercultural world: foreign language education as cultural politics*. Multilingual Matters.

Gumperz, J. (1992). Contextualization and understanding. In Duranti, A. & Goodwin, C. (Eds.), *Rethinking context: language as an interactive phenomenon*, 229–253. Cambridge University Press.

Hall, S. (1991). Old and new identities, old and new ethnicities. In King, A. D. (Ed.), *Culture, globalisation and the world-system*, 40–68. Palgrave.

Hall, S. (1996a). The question of cultural identity. In Hall, S., Held, D., Hubert, D. & Thompson, K. (Eds.), *Modernity: an introduction to modern societies*, 595–634. Blackwell.

Hall, S. (1996b). The West and the Rest: discourse and power. In Hall, S., Held, D., Hubert, D. & Thompson, K. (Eds.), *Modernity: an introduction to modern societies*, 184–228. Blackwell.

Harré, R. & Van Langenhove, L. (1999). Introducing positioning theory. In Harré, R. & Van Langenhove, L. (Eds.), *Positioning theory*, 14–31. Blackwell.

Hawad, M. (1987). *Caravane de la Soif*. Elisud.

Henriksen, T. D. (2008). Liquidating roles and crystallising positions: investigating the road between role and positioning theory. In Moghaddam, F. M., Harré, R. & Lee, N. (Eds.), *Global conflict resolution through positioning analysis*, 41–64. Springer.

Hervik, P. (2013). Racism, neo-racism. In ENAR (Ed.), *Recycling hatred: racism(s) in Europe today: a dialogue between academics, equality experts and civil society activists*, 43–52. The European Network Against Racism.

Hester, S. & Eglin, P. (1996). Membership categorization analysis: an introduction. In Hester, S. & Eglin, P. (Eds.), *Culture in action: studies in membership categorization analysis*, 1–24. University Press of America.

Hester, S. & Hester, S. (2012). Categorial occasionality and transformation: analyzing culture in action. *Human Studies* 35, 4, 563–581.

Holliday, A. R. (2010). Complexity in cultural identity. *Language & Intercultural Communication* 10, 2, 165–177.

Holliday, A. R. (2011). *Intercultural communication and ideology*. Sage.

Holliday, A. R. (2016a). Cultural travel and cultural prejudice. In Aquino, M. B. & Frota, S. (Eds.), *Identities: representation and practices*, 25–44. CELGA-ILTEC, University of Coimbra.

Holliday, A. R. (2016b). Difference and awareness in cultural travel: negotiating blocks and threads. *Language and Intercultural Communication* 16, 3, 318–331.

Holliday, A. R. (2016c). Revisiting intercultural competence: small culture formation on the go through threads of experience. *International Journal of Bias, Identity & Diversities in Education* 1, 2, 1–13.

Holliday, A. R. (2018a). Designing a course in intercultural education. *Intercultural Communication Education* 1, 1, 3–10.

Holliday, A. R. (2018b). Native-speakerism. In Liontas, J. (Ed.), *TESOL Encyclopedia of English Language Teaching*. Wiley.

Holliday, A. R. (2018c). *Understanding intercultural communication: negotiating a grammar of culture*. 2nd ed. Routledge.

Holliday, A. R. & MacDonald, M. N. (2019). Researching the intercultural: intersubjectivity and the problem with postpositivism. *Applied Linguistics*, 1–20.

hooks, b. (1984). *Feminist theory: from margin to center*. South End Press.

Kamal, A. (2015). Interrogating assumptions of native-speakerism from the perspective of Kuwait university English language students. In Swan, A., Aboshiha, P. J. & Holliday, A. R. (Eds.), *(En)countering native-speakerism: global perspectives*, 124–140. Palgrave.

Kubota, R. (2003). Unfinished knowledge: the story of Barbara. *College ESL* 10, 1–2, 84–92.

Kubota, R. (2016). The multi/plural turn, postcolonial theory, and neoliberal multiculturalism: complicities and implications for applied linguistics. *Applied Linguistics* 37, 4, 474–494.

Kuhn, T. (1970). *The structure of scientific revolutions*. University of Chicago Press.

Kumaravadivelu, B. (2007). *Cultural globalization and language education*. Yale University Press.

Kumaravadivelu, B. (2012). Individual identity, cultural globalisation, and teaching English as an international language: the case for an epistemic break. In Alsagoff, L., Renandya, W., Hu, G. & McKay, S. (Eds.), *Principles and practices for teaching English as an international language*, 9–27. Routledge.

Lalami, L. (2015). *The Moor's account*. Kindle ed. Periscope.

Latour, B. (1988). The politics of explanation: an alternative. In Woolgar, S. (Ed.), *Knowledge and reflexivity, new frontiers in the sociology of knowledge*, 155–177. Sage.

Lyotard, J.-F. (1979). *The postmodern condition: a report on knowledge*. Manchester University Press.

MacDonald, M. N. (2017). *Interrogating the 'third space': The discourse of hybridity in intercultural studies*. Paper presented at the International Association of Language & Intercultural Communication Annual Conference, 'Third Space': Negotiating meaning and performing 'culture', Edinburgh Napier University.

MacDonald, M. N. & O'Regan, J. P. (2011). A global agenda for intercultural communication research and practice. In Jackson, J. (Ed.), *Routledge handbook of language and intercultural communication*, 553–567. Routledge.

Mannheim, K. (1936). *Ideology and utopia.* Harcourt, Brace & Company.

McAdams, D. P. & Logan, R. L. (2006). Creative work, love, and the dialectic in selected life stories of academics. In McAdams, D. P., Josselson, R. & Lieblich, A. (Eds.), *Identity and story: creating self in narrative*, 89–108. American Psychological Association.

McQueen, S. (2013). *Twelve years a slave.* Summit Entertainment.

Merrill, B. & West, L. (2009). *Using biographical methods in social research.* Sage.

Merton, A. & Rebcher, N. (2017). *No roots.* Paper Plane Records.

Merton, R. K. (1972). Insiders and outsiders: a chapter in the sociology of knowledge. *Amdercan Journal of Sociology* 78, 1, 9–47.

Miller, E. R. (2011). Indeterminacy and interview research: co-constructing ambiguity and clarity in interviews with an adult immigrant learner of English. *Applied Linguistics* 32, 1, 43–59.

Mills, C. W. (1970). *The sociological imagination.* Pelican.

Osmond, J. & Roed, J. (2009). Sometimes it means more work ... In Jones, E. (Ed.), *Internationalisation and the student voice: higher education perspectives*, 113–124. Routledge.

Roy, A. (2002). Come September: in conversation with Howard Zinn [Audio recording]. Santa Fe: Lensing Performing Arts Centre, Lannan Foundation.

Sacks, H. (1992). *Lectures on conversation*, Volume 2. Blackwell.

Said, E. (1978). *Orientalism.* Routledge & Kegan Paul.

Sardar, Z. (2009). *Balti Britain: a journey through the British Asian experience.* Kindle ed. Granta.

Sawyer, L. & Jones, P. (2008). Voices of migrants: solidarity and resistance. In Delanty, G., Wodak, R. & Jones, P. (Eds.), *Identity, belonging and migration*, 241–260. Liverpool University Press.

Somers, M. R. (1994). The narrative constitution of identity: a rational and network approach. *Theory and Society* 23, 605–649.

Stenhouse, L. (1985). The illuminative research tradition. In Ruddock, J. & Hopkins, D. (Eds.), *Research as a basis for teaching: readings from the work of Lawrence Stenhouse*, 3132. Heinemann.

Talmy, S. (2011). The interview as collaborative achievement: interaction, identity, and ideology in a speech event. *Applied Linguistics* 32, 1, 25–42.

Wallace, C. (2011). A school of immigrants: how new arrivals become pupils in a multilingual London school. *Language and Intercultural Communication* 11, 2, 97–112.

Weber, M. (1964). *The theory of social and economic organisation.* The Free Press.

Weber, M. (1968). Ideal types and theory construction. In Brodbeck, M. (Ed.), *Readings in the philosophy of the social sciences*, 496–507. Macmillan.

Wenger, E. (2000). Communities of practice and social learning systems. *Organization* 7, 2, 225–246.

Wodak, R. & Meyer, M. (2015). Critical discourse studies: history, agenda, theory and methodology. In Wodak, R. & Meyer, M. (Eds.), *Methods or critical discourse studies*, 3rd ed., 2–22. Sage.

Wolff, S. (2004). Ways into the field and their variants. In Flick, U., von Kardoff, E. & Steinke, I. (Eds.), *A companion to qualitative research*, 195–202. Sage.

Yamchi, N. (2015). 'I am not what you think I am': EFL undergraduates' experience of academic writing, facing discourses of formulaic writing. In Swan, A., Aboshiha, P. J. & Holliday, A. R. (Eds.), *(En)countering native-speakerism: global perspectives*, 177–192. Palgrave.

Young, T. & Sercombe, P. (2010). Communication, discourses and interculturality. *Language & Intercultural Communication* 10, 3, 181–188.

Index

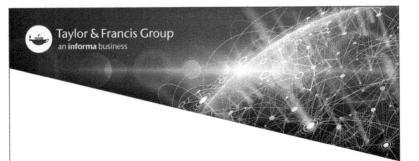